Astral Worship

by

J. H. Hill, M. D.

"Now, what I want is--facts."--_Boz._

CONTENTS.

INTRODUCTION

THE GEOCENTRIC SYSTEM OF NATURE

The Earth

The Firmament

The Planets

The Constellations 15 The Zodiac

THE SACRED NUMBERS 7 AND 12

THE TWELVE THOUSAND YEAR CYCLE

THE ANCIENT TRIAD

GOD SOL

THE ANCIENT COSMOGONY

FALL AND REDEMPTION OF MAN

INCARNATIONS OF GOD SOL

FABLE OF THE TWELVE LABORS

ANNIVERSARIES OF SOLAR WORSHIP

The Nativity 40 Epiphany or Twelfth Day

Lent or Lenten Season

Passion Week

Passion Plays

Resurrection and Easter Festival

Annunciation

Ascension

Assumption

The Lord's Supper

Transubstantiation

Autumnal Crucifixion

Michaelmas

PERSONIFICATIONS OF THE DIVISIONS OF TIME

The Hours

The Days

The Months

The Seasons

Half Year of Increasing Days

Half Year of Decreasing Days

Last Quarter of the Year

ZODIACAL SYMBOLS OF SOLAR WORSHIP

The Sphinx

The Dragon

The Bull

The Ram The Lamb

The Fish

SIGNS OF THE CROSS

FUTURE REWARDS AND PUNISHMENTS

The Oriental System

The Occidental System

The Second or General Judgment

JEWISH, OR ANCIENT CHRISTIANITY

THE PROPHECIES

ROMAN OR MODERN CHRISTIANITY

FREEMASONRY AND DRUIDISM

THE SABBATH

PIOUS FRAUDS

CONCLUSION

INTRODUCTION.

In an article, entitled "Then and Now," published in the December number, 1890, of "The Arena," its author, a distinguished Unitarian D.D. of Boston, Mass., says. "Astronomy has shattered the fallacies of Astrology; and people have found out that the stars are minding their own business instead of meddling with theirs." Now, while it is true that modern Astronomy has superseded the ancient system, and people have ceased to believe that the stars are intervening in mundane affairs, nothing could be further from the truth than the assertion that "Astronomy has shattered the fallacies of Astrology;" and those of our readers who will accord to this work an unprejudiced perusal can hardly fail to be convinced that a large majority of the people of Christendom are dominated as much by these fallacies as were our Pagan ancestry--the only difference being a change of name. The dogmatic element of religion, which was anciently designated as Astrology, is now known as Theology.

All the evidences bearing upon the subject indicate that the founders of the primary form of religion were a sect of philosophers, known as Magi, or wise men, of the Aryan race of Central Asia, who, having lived ages before any conceptions of the supernatural had obtained in the world, and speculating relative to the "beginnings of things," were necessarily confined to the contemplation and study of nature, the elements of which they believed to be self-existent and endless in duration; but, being wholly without knowledge of her inherent forces, they explained her manifold processes by conceiving the idea that she was animated by a great and inherent soul or spirit, emanations from which impressed all her parts with life and motion. Thus, endowing man, and other animals, with souls emanating alike from the imaginary great soul of nature, they believed, and taught, that immediately after death all souls were absorbed into their source, where, as "the dewdrop slips into the shining sea," all personal identity was forever lost. Hence we see that although recognizing the soul as immortal, considering it, not as an entity existing independent of matter, but as the spirit of matter itself, the primary religion was the exponent of the purest form of Materialism.

[handwritten margin notes: simplest religious forms as being earliest form of materialism? Paganism]

Being the Astronomers of their day, and mistaking the apparent for the real, the ancient Magi constructed that erroneous system of nature known as the Geocentric, and, in conformity thereto, composed a collection of Astronomical Allegories, in which the emanations from the imaginary great soul of nature, by which they believed all materialities we're impressed with life and motion, were personified and made to play their respective parts. Basing the religion they instituted upon their system of Allegorical Astronomy, and making its personifications the objects of worship, they thus originated the anthropomorphic or man-like Gods, and, claiming to have composed them under the inspiration of these self same divinities, they designated them as sacred records, or Scriptures, and taught the ignorant masses that they were literal histories, and their personifications real personages, who, having once lived upon earth, and; for the

[handwritten margin notes: all materials that fascinated us we personified → anthropomorphic Gods ↓ stories as literal histories]

good of mankind, performed the wondrous works imputed to them, were then in heaven whence they came.

Thus we see that the primary religion, which is popularly known as Paganism, was founded in the worship of personified nature; that, according special homage to the imaginary genii of the stars, and inculcating supreme adoration to the divinity supposed to reside in the sun, it was anciently known by the general name of Astrolatry, and by the more specific one of solar worship; and that its founders, arrogating to themselves the title of Astrologers, gave to its dogmatic element the name of Astrology.

In studying the primitive forms of religion it will be found that none of them taught anything relative to a future life, for the simple reason that their founders had no conceptions of such a state. Hence it follows that the laws they enacted were intended solely for the regulation of their social relations, and, to secure their observance, they were embodied into their sacred records and made part of their religion. One form of that most ancient worship was known as Sabaism, or Sabism. Another form of the same religion was the Ancient Judaism, as portrayed in the Old Testament, and more especially in the Pentateuch, or first five books; in the Decalogue of which the only promise made for the observance of one of the Commandments is length of days on earth; and, in a general summing up of the blessings and curses to be enjoyed or suffered, for the observance or violation of the laws, as recorded in the 28th chapter of Deuteronomy, it will be seen they are all of a temporal character only. At the beginning of the Christian era there were still in existence a sect of Jews known as Sadducees, who were strict adherents to the primitive form of worship, and their belief relative to the state of the dead we find recorded in Ecclesiastes xii., 7, which reads: "Then shall the dust return to earth as it was, and the spirit shall return to God who gave it."

For ages the doctrine of soul absorption, immediately after death, constituted the belief of mankind; but ultimately recognizing the fact that the temporal punishments of the existing laws were wholly inadequate to the prevention of crime, and conceiving the idea that the ignorant and vicious masses could be governed with a surer hand by appealing to the sentiments of hope and fear in relation to the rewards and punishments of an imaginary future life, the ancient Astrologers resolved to remodel the dogmatic elements of religion so as to include that doctrine. But realizing the necessity, of suppressing the belief in the absorption of all souls, immediately after death, they ceased to teach it, and ultimately it was embodied in that secret and unwritten system known as the Esoteric philosophy, in which the Astrologers formulated their own private belief, and which for many centuries was kept from the knowledge of the uninitiated by their successors in the priestly office. As they were the sole custodians of the Scriptures, they made do change in their verbiage, but, adding the doctrine of future rewards and punishments to that written and openly taught system of faith known as the Exoteric creed, they made it the more impressive by instituting a system of imposing rites and ceremonies, which they designated as Mysteries, into which they initiated the neophytes, and in which were portrayed, in the most vivid manner, the rewards and punishments of the imaginary future life, which they taught were the awards of the Gods for the observance or violation of the laws. These teachings were inculcated in the lesser degrees only, but those who were found worthy of so great a distinction were also inducted into the higher degrees, in which was imparted the knowledge of the Esoteric philosophy. In both the lesser and higher degrees the initiates received instruction in an oral manner only; and all were bound by the most fearful oaths not to reveal the secrets imparted to them.

Thus were the votaries of the ancient Astral worship divided into two distinct classes, the Esoterics, or Gnostics; and the Exoterics, or Agnostics; the former comprising those who knew that the Gods were mythical and the scriptures allegorical; and the latter, those who were taught that the Gods were real, and the scriptures historical; or, in other words, it was philosophy for the cultured few, and religion for the ignorant multitude. The initiates into the secrets of these two systems recognized them as the two Gospels; and Paul must have had reference to them in his Epistle to the Galatians ii., 2, where he distinguishes the Gospel which he preached on ordinary occasions from that Gospel which he preached "privately to them which were of reputation."

Such was the system of Astrolatry, which, originating in the Orient, and becoming, after being remodelled in Egypt, the prototype of all Occidental forms of worship, was recognized, successively, as the state religion of the Grecian and Roman Empires; and we propose to describe the erroneous system of nature upon which it was based, and to develop the origins of its cycles, dogmas, ordinances, anniversaries, personifications and symbols, with the view to proving that it was the very same system which was ultimately perpetuated under the name of Christianity. We also propose to present the origins and abridged histories of its two forms, the Jewish, or ancient, and the Roman, or modern; and to give an account of the conflict between the votaries of the latter, and the adherents to the established form of worship, which culminated in the fourth century in the substitution of Christianity as the state religion of the Roman Empire. We furthermore propose to show the changes to which the creed and scriptures were subjected during the Middle Ages, and at the Reformation in the sixteenth century, through which they assumed the phases as now taught in the theologies, respectively of Catholicism and Orthodox Protestantism. We also present an article relative to Freemasonry and Druidism, for the purpose of showing that, primarily, they were but different forms of the ancient Astrolatry. We also devote a few pages to the subjects of the Sabbath, and to that of "Pious Frauds."

Note.--For the matter published in this work, we are principally indebted to the writings of Robert Taylor, an erudite but recusant minister of the church of England, who flourished about seventy years ago, and who, being too honest to continue to preach what, after thorough investigation, he did not believe, began to give expression to his doubts by writing and lecturing. Not being able to cope with his arguments, the clergy, under the charge of the impossible crime of blasphemy, had him imprisoned for more than two years, during which time he wrote his great work entitled "The Diegesis," which should be read by all persons who are investigating the claim of the Christian religion to Divine authenticity.

THE GEOCENTRIC SYSTEM OF NATURE.

In constructing their system of nature, the ancient
Astronomers constituted it of the Earth, the
Firmament, the Planets, the Constellations and the
Zodiac, and we will refer to them in the order
named.

The Earth.

Believing that the earth was the only world, that it
was a vast circular plane, and that it was the fixed
and immovable center around which revolved the
celestial luminaries, the ancient Astronomers, in
conformity to the requirement of the doctrine of
future rewards and punishments, as inculcated in
the Egyptian Version of the Exoteric Creed, divided
it into an upper and an under, or nether world,
which they connected by a sinuous and tenebrious
passage.

The Firmament.

The azure dome, called the firmament in the book
of Genesis, was believed to be a solid transparency,
which we find described, in the fourth chapter and
sixth verse, of that collection of Astronomical
Allegories, called the Apocalypse, or Book of
Revelation, "as a sea of glass like unto crystal." It
was represented as being supported by four pillars,
resting upon the earth, one at each of the cardinal
points, which were designated as "the pillars of
heaven." Conceiving the idea that there were
windows in the firmament, the ancient Astronomers
called them "the windows of heaven" and taught

that they were opened when it rained, and closed when it ceased to rain. Hence it is evident that the ancient Astronomers did not refer to these pillars and windows in a figurative sense, but as real appurtenances to a solid firmament, as will be seen by reference to Gen. vii. 11, and viii. 2, Job xxvi. 11, and Malachi iii. 10.

The Planets.

Believing that the stars were but mere flambeaux, suspended beneath the firmament, and revolving round the earth, for the sole purpose of giving it light and heat; and observing that seven of these, answering to the Sun, Moon, Mercury, Venus, Mars, Jupiter and Saturn, had perceptible movements, in relation to the other luminaries, the ancient astronomers designated them as planets or wandering stars.

The Constellations.

Perceiving that the other celestial luminaries maintained the same relation to each other, and designating them as fixed stars, the ancient astronomers grouped those visible to them into forty-eight Constellations; and giving names to these, they also attached names to the stars of larger magnitude, which was done for the purpose of locating and distinguishing them with greater ease.

The Zodiac.

Through twelve of these Constellations, mostly contained within a belt of 16 degrees in width, and within which the planets appeared to revolve, the ancient astronomers inscribed a central line representing the Ecliptic, or apparent orbit of the sun, which they divided into 360 degrees; and quartering these to denote the seasons, they named the cardinal points the Summer and Winter Solstices, and the Vernal and Autumnal Equinoxes; the former referring to the longest and shortest days of the year; and the latter to the two periods when the days and nights are equal. An abbreviatory sign having been attached to each of these constellations, the great celestial belt containing them was called "the wheel of the signs," or "a wheel in the middle of a wheel," as designated by that old Astrologer, Ezekiel the Prophet, in chap. i. and 16th verse. But for the reason that, with only one exception, the forms of living things, either real or mythical, were given to them, this belt, ultimately, wad designated as the Zodiac; or Circle of living Creatures, see Ezekiel, chap. i. Constituting the essential feature of the ancient Astronomy, we present, in our frontispiece, a diagram of the Zodiac, as anciently represented, to which, as well as to Burritts' Celestial Atlas, our readers will be necessitated to make frequent reference.

Recent researches among the ruins of ancient cities have developed the fact that several centuries before the beginning of our era the astronomers had invented the telescope, and discovered the true or heliocentric system of nature; but for the reason that religion had been based upon the false, or geocentric system, it was deemed prudent not to teach it to the masses. Hence, hiding it away among the other secrets of the Esoteric philosophy, the knowledge of it was lost during the Middle Ages; and when rediscovered, the hierarchy of the Church of Rome, upon the plea that it was contrary to the teachings of Scripture, resorted to inquisitorial tortures to suppress its promulgation; but, in spite of all their efforts, it has been universally accepted; and, in this otherwise enlightened age, we have presented to us the anomaly of a religion based upon a false system of Astronomy, while its votaries believe in the true system.

THE SACRED NUMBERS 7 AND 12.

In reference to the planets, and the signs of the Zodiac, the numbers seven and twelve were recognized as sacred by the ancient Astrologers, and dedications were made to them in all kinds and sorts of forms. In the allegories, the genii of the planets were designated as spirits or messengers to the Supreme Deity, imaginarily enthroned above the firmament, which we find described in Revelations iv. 5, as "Seven lamps of fire burning before the throne, which are the seven spirits of God;" and which were represented by lights burning in seven branched candlesticks set before the altars in the temples; the central light for the Sun; the Moon, Mercury and Venus on one side; and Mars, Jupiter and Saturn on the other. The seven branched candlesticks seen in all Catholic churches, and in some Protestant ones, are intended to represent the same planetary system.

Among the numerous dedications to the genii of the planets we mention the seven days of the week, the seven stories of the tower of Babylon, the seven gates of Thebes, the seven piped flute of Pan, the seven stringed lyre of Apollo, the seven books of fate, the book of seven seals, the seven castes into which the Egyptians and East Indians were divided, and the jubilee of seven times seven years. Among the dedications to the twelve signs we mention the twelve months of the year, the grand cycle of 12,000 years, the twelve altars of James, the twelve labors of Hercules, the twelve divisions of the Egyptian Labyrinth, the twelve shields of Mars, the twelve precious stones, ranged in threes to denote the seasons, in the breastplate of High Priest, the twelve foundations of the Sacred City, referred to in the Book of Revelation, the twelve sons of Jacob, the twelve tribes of Israel, and the twelve Disciples. In the Book of Revelation alone the number 7 is repeated twenty-four times, and the number 12 fourteen times.

THE TWELVE THOUSAND YEAR CYCLE.

In determining the duration of the period within which were to occur the events taught in the doctrines of the Exoteric Creed, the ancient Astrologers dedicated a thousand years to each of the signs of the Zodiac, and thus inaugurating the cycle of twelve thousand years, taught that, at its conclusion, the heaven and the earth, which they believed to be composed of the indestructible elements of fire, air, earth and water, would, through the agency of the first of these, be reduced to chaos, as a preliminary to the reorganization of a new heaven and a new earth at the beginning of the succeeding cycle. Such was the origin of the grand cycle of the ancient Astrolatry, and it must be borne in mind that its authors made its conclusion to correspond in time and circumstance to the doctrines relating to the finale of the plan of redemption.

THE ANCIENT TRIAD.

After conceiving the idea of a primeval chaos, constituted of four indestructible elements of which fire was the leading one, the Oriental astrologers began to indulge in speculations relative to the agencies which were engaged in its organization. Having no knowledge of the forces inherent in nature, they imputed this work to three intelligences, which, embodying the All in All, they personified by the figure of a man with three heads, and to this trinity gave the names of Brahma, Vishnu and Siva. Such a figure, carved in stone, may be seen in the island Cave of Elephanta, near Bombay, India, and is popularly believed to represent the Creator, Preserver and Destroyer; but, in determining their true signification, we must be governed by the ancient teachings that "All things were made by one god-head with three names, and this God is all things." Hence the conclusion is

irresistible that the first person represents neither
the creator nor organizer of chaos, but chaos itself;
the second person, its organizer and governor; and
the third person, the agent in nature which
impresses all her parts with life and motion; the
latter being the imaginary great soul or spirit
inculcated in the Esoteric philosophy. In support of
this opinion it will be found that the Egyptian Triad
of Father, Son and Spirit is virtually the same we
have assigned to its Oriental prototype. Thus we see
that to the ancient Astrolatry Christendom is
indebted for the Trinity of

"God the Father, God the Son, God the Spirit--three
in one."

But, having ascribed supreme intelligence or reason
to its second person, under the name of the Logos,
or Word, and designating its third person as the
Holy Ghost, the ancient Triad was usually
formulated as the Father, the Word and the Holy
Ghost, as may be seen by reference to the text in the
allegories which we find recorded in I John v. 7,
which reads that "There are three that bear record in
heaven, the Father, the Word and the Holy Ghost,
and these three are one."

Considered in some forms of Astrolatry as too
sacred to attach a name to the triune Deity, he was
called "the One," and we find him thus designated
in the 4th chapter of Revelation, where, like Zeus
and Jupiter, of the Grecian and Roman mythologies,
he is represented as seated above the firmament,
upon a throne from which "proceeded lightnings
and thunderings," and to whom all, the subordinate

divinities were made to pay homage. As the hurler of thunderbolts he was called "the Thunderer," and as the opener of the windows of heaven, when it rained, he was designated "Jupiter Pluvius." Such was the ancient Triad made to say of himself, in an inscription found in the ruins of the temple at Sais in Egypt, "I am all that has been, all that is, and all that shall be, and no mortal has lifted yet the veil that covers me;" and such was the Triunity referred to as the God Universe by Pliny, the Roman philosopher and naturalist, who, flourishing in the first century of the Christian era, wrote that he is "An infinite God which has never been created, and which shall never come to an end. To look for something else beyond it is useless labor for man and out of his reach. Behold that truly sacred Being, eternal and immense, which includes within itself everything; it is All in All, or rather itself is All. It is the work of nature, and itself is nature."

Thus we see that, although inculcating homage to a multitude of subordinate divinities, the ancient Astrolatry was only an apparent Polytheism; its enlightened votaries, recognizing the dogma of the unity of God, were in reality Monotheists, paying supreme adoration to the mythical genius of the Sun, to whom we will now direct attention.

GOD SOL.

In determining the characteristics of the supreme divinity of astral worship, it must be borne in mind that its founders taught that he was evolved or engendered by the Father, or first person in the sacred Triad, from his pure substance, which as we have shown was constituted of chaos or the primeval fire into which they supposed all things were reduced through the agency of that element at the conclusion of 12,000 year cycles. Hence, designating that mythical being as the only begotten of the Father, they personified him as God the Son, or second person in the sacred Triad; and recognizing the Sun as the ruling star, very appropriately made him the presiding genius of that luminary, under the title of God Sol. According homage to light as his chief attribute, he is referred to in the allegories as "The true Light, which lighteth every man that cometh into the world," John i., 9; and, although designated as the only begotten of the Father, his co-existence with him, under the title of the Logos or Word, is shown in the text which reads, "In the beginning was the Word, and the Word was with God, and the Word was God," John i., 1.

Personifying the principles of Good and Evil in God Sol, the ancient Astrologers consecrated the six divisions of the 12,000 year cycle, corresponding to the reproductive months of Spring and Summer, to him as Lord of Good, and symbolizing him by the constellation of the Zodiac in which the Vernal Equinox successively occurred, as explained hereafter, they dedicated the six divisions of that cycle, corresponding to the destructive months of Autumn and Winter, to him as Lord of Evil, and as such, symbolizing him by the serpent, marked the beginning of his reign by the constellation "Serpens," placed in conjunction with the Autumnal

Equinox. Personifying in him the opposing principles of Good and Evil, he was to the ancients both God and Devil, or the varied God, who, in relation to the seasons, was described as beautiful in Spring, powerful in Summer, beneficent in Autumn and terrible in Winter. Thus under various names, intended to represent God Sol in relation to the diversified seasons, we find recorded in the Scriptures, or solar fables, numerous portrayals of imaginary conflicts, in which the Evil principle, triumphing during Autumn and Winter, is conquered at the Vernal Equinox by the Good principle, who, bringing back equal days and nights, restores the harmony of nature.

The eternal enmity between the principles of Good and Evil, as manifested in the diversity of the seasons, we find portrayed in the Constellations Hercules and Draco, placed in the northern heavens, in which the heel of the former, representing one of the most ancient of the imaginary incarnations of God Sol, to which we will refer hereafter, is resting upon the head of the latter, as referred to in Genesis iii., 15, which makes God Sol, or the Lord God, say to the serpent, "I will put enmity between thee and the woman, and between thy seed and her seed; it shall bruise thy head, and thou shalt bruise his heel." The woman alluded to in this text is the Virgo of the Zodiac, as will be made apparent hereafter.

Of all the divinities of the ancient mythology God Sol was the only one distinguished by the exalted title of Lord or Lord God, for the reason that he was made the organizer of chaos and governor of heaven and earth. Hence, having constituted him the lord of light and darkness, as well as good and evil, the ancient astrologers in composing the solar fables made him say of himself, "I form the light and create darkness; I make peace and create evil, I the Lord do all these things," Isaiah xlv., 7. "Shall there be evil in a city, and the Lord hath not done it?" Amos iii., 6. Besides the title of Lord or Lord God, the solar divinity is also designated in the allegories as the Lord of Lords and the King of Kings, the Invincible, the Mighty God, etc.

Subjecting the mythical genius of the sun, in his apparent annual revolution round the earth, to the four stages of human life from infancy to old age, the ancient Magi fixed the natal day of the young God Sol at the winter solstice, the Virgo of the Zodiac was made his mother, and the constellation in conjunction with her, which is now known as Bootes, but anciently called Arcturus, his foster father. He is represented as holding in leash two hunting dogs and driving Ursa Major, or the Great Bear, around the north pole, thus showing that the original occupation of the celestial foster father of the young God Sol was that of a bear driver, and that his sons, referred to in job xxxviii., 32, are the dogs Asterion and Chara. It will be observed that Virgo is represented in our illustration with a child in her arms, for the reason that she is so represented in the ancient Zodiacs, and the fact will be readily conceded that she is the only Virgin who could give birth to a child and be a virgin still.

THE ANCIENT COSMOGONY.

Speculating relative to the order in which chaos had
been organized, the ancient Astrologers constructed
a Cosmogony, which divided the labors of God the
Son, or second person in the Trinity, into six
periods of a thousand years each; and which,
answering to the six divisions of the 12,000 year
cycle corresponding to the reproductive months of
Spring and Summer, taught that in the first period
he made the earth; in the second, the firmament; in
the third, vegetation; in the fourth, the Sun and
Moon and "the stars also;" in the fifth, the animals,
fishes, birds, etc., and in the sixth, Man.

That vegetation was made before the Sun was not
an inconsistent idea to the originators of the ancient
Cosmogony. They imagined that the heat and light,
emanating from the elementary fire, were sufficient
to stimulate its growth, after which God the Son
gathered it together and made the Celestial
luminaries. In the solar fables this imaginary
element is called the fire-ether, or sacred fire of the
stars.

FALL AND REDEMPTION OF MAN.

Religion having been based upon the worship of
personified nature, it is evident that its founders
fabricated its dogmatic element from their
conceptions of her destructive and reproductive
processes as manifested in the rotation and diversity
of the seasons. The apparent retreat of the sun from

the earth, in winter, and his return in the spring, suggesting the idea of a figurative death and resurrection of the genius of that luminary, they applied these phenomena of the year to man, and composed the allegories relative to his fall and redemption, as inculcated in the Exoteric Creed. In the allegory relating to the fall, it was taught that, after making the first human pair, the Lord of Good or the Lord God placed them in a beautiful garden-- corresponding to the seasons of fruits and flowers or months of Spring and Summer, with the injunction, under a, penalty, not to eat of the fruit of a certain tree. When the Lord of Evil, or Devil, symbolized by the serpent and represented by the constellation "Serpens" placed in conjunction with the Autumnal Equinox, meeting them on the confines of his dominion, and tempting the woman, and she the man, they ate of the forbidden fruit; thus, falling from their first estate, and committing the original sin, they involved the whole human race in the consequences of their disobedience. Then the Lord God, pronouncing a curse against the serpent, clothed the man and woman with skins to protect them against the inclemency of his, dominion as Lord of Evil, and drove them from the garden; after which they were necessitated to earn their bread by tilling the ground.

In, reference to the plan of redemption, the ancient Astrologers divided the 6,000 years appropriated to man, as the duration of his race on earth, into ten equal cycles, and taught that at the conclusion of each God Sol, as Lord of Good, would manifest himself in the flesh, to destroy his works as Lord of Evil, and through suffering and death make an atonement for sin. Thus having originated the doctrines of original sin, incarnation and vicarious atonement, as parts of the plan of redemption, and making its finale correspond, in point of time, to the conclusion of the 12,000 year cycle, their successors in the priestly office ultimately inculcated the additional dogmas of the general judgment and future rewards and punishments, as we have shown in our introduction.

Having based the fables of the fall and redemption of man upon the idea that he was impelled, without his volition, to pass from the dominion of God to that of the Devil, or in other words, upon his subjection to the inexorable necessity which makes the inclement seasons of Autumn and Winter succeed the beneficent ones of Spring and Summer, its authors composed the original of the text which, found in Romans viii., 20, reads that "The creature was made subject to vanity (Evil), not willingly, but by reason of him who hath subjected the same in hope."

But for the popular teaching in favor of its being literal history, no one could read the account of the fall of man, as recorded in the third chapter of Genesis, without recognizing it as simply an allegory; or fail to realize, the force of the argument of no fall, no redemption, and if no redemption, no God to reward or Devil to punish; no hell to suffer, or heaven to enjoy. The fact is that these are but antithetical ideas which came in together, and must survive or perish together. They cannot be separated without destroying the whole theological fabric.

INCARNATIONS OF GOD SOL.

Believing that God Sol was necessitated to remain
at his post to direct the course of the sun, the
ancient astrologers conceived the idea of teaching
that, attended by a retinue of subordinate genii, he
descended to earth through the medium of
incarnations at the end of 600 year cycles, to
perform the work of man's redemption and, having
made Virgo of the Zodiac the mother of the Solar
divinity, they taught in their allegorical Astronomy,
or scriptures, that his incarnations were born of a
Virgin. Hence we find that God Sol, usually
designated by the title of the Word, "was made
flesh, and dwelt among us." John i., 14.

In a discourse upon this text delivered by Tillotson,
Archbishop of Canterbury, in the year 1680,
published in the fourth volume of Woodhouse's
edition of his Grace's sermons, in the year 1744,
concerning the Incarnation of our blessed Saviour,
he explains the necessity of incarnation by saying
that "There was likewise a great inclination in
mankind to the worship of a visible Deity, so God
was pleased to appear in our nature, that they, who
were so fond of a visible Deity, might have one,
even a true and natural image of God the Father, the
express image of his person." It only requires a little
reflection to appreciate the Prelate's covert irony
and want of faith.

Having ascribed to the imaginary incarnations of
God Sol the characteristics of heaven-descending,
virgin-born, earth-walking, wonder-working, dying,
resuscitated and ascending sons of God, the ancient

Astrologers attached to them the several titles of
Saviour, Redeemer, Avatar, Divine-Helper, Shiloh,
Messiah, Christ; and, in reference to their foster-
father, that of Son of Man. Teaching that they
continued to make intercession for sin, after their
ascension to the right hand of the Father, they were
also called Intercessors, Mediators or Advocates
with the Father. From teaching their appearance
every 600 years originated the Egyptian legend of
the Phoenix, a bird said to descend from the sun at
these intervals, and, after being consumed upon the
altar in the temple of On, or city of the sun--called
Heliopolis by the Greeks--would rise from its ashes
and ascend to its source. According to the civil laws
of Egypt, manhood was not attained until the age of
thirty years. Hence the earthly mission of incarnate
Saviours was made to begin at that age; and for the
reason that, relating to the apparent transit of the
sun through the twelve signs of the Zodiac, it was
completed during the period of one year.

To impress the ignorant masses with the belief that
the scriptures were literal histories, and the
incarnate Saviours real personages, the ancient
Astrologers caused tombs to be erected in which it
was claimed they were buried. Such sepulchres
were erected to Hercules at Cadiz, to Apollo at
Delphi, and to other Saviours at many other places,
to which their respective votaries were induced to
perform pilgrimages. In Egypt the pyramids were
built, partly for astronomical purposes, and partly as
tombs for Saviours, claimed to have been kings,
who had once ruled over the country; and why
should we not recognize that magnificent structure
known as the Church of the Holy Sepulchre, at

Jerusalem, as but another of those tombs of
Saviours in which no Saviour was ever entombed?

Thus we have shown that it was God Sol, the only
begotten of the Father, or second person in the
sacred Triad, to whom supreme adoration was
inculcated in all forms of the ancient Astrolatry; and
that its cultured votaries, understanding that the
doctrines pertaining to the fall and redemption of
man were evolved from the figurative death and
resurrection of the solar divinity, recognized the
doctrine of incarnation as a priestly invention
intended only for the ignorant masses.

FABLE OF THE TWELVE LABORS.

The authors of the original solar fables, having
lived in that remote age in which physical prowess
was recognized as the highest attribute of humanity,
conceived the idea that God Sol, while passing
through his apparent orbit, had to fight his way with
the animals of the Zodiac, and with others in
conjunction with them. Hence, designating him as
the Mighty Hunter, and calling his exploits the
twelve labors, they made the incarnate Saviours the
heroes of similar ones on earth, which they taught
were performed for the good of mankind; and that,
after fulfilling their earthly mission, they were
exhaled to heaven through the agency of fire. When
these fables were composed the Summer Solstice
was in the sign of Leo, and making the twelve
labors begin in it, the first consisted in the killing of
a lion, and the second, in rescuing a virgin (Virgo)

by the destruction of a Hydra, the constellation in
conjunction with her. Upon one of the Assyrian
marbles on exhibition in the British Museum these
two labors are represented as having been
performed by a saviour by the name of Nimroud. In
the constellations of Taurus, the bull of the Zodiac,
and of Orion, originally known as Horns, in
conjunction therewith, we have groupings of stars
representing the latter as one of the mighty hunters
of the ancient Astrolatry, supporting on his left arm
the shield of the lion's skin, the trophy of the first
labor, and holding a club in his uplifted right hand,
is engaged in performing the tenth labor by a
conflict with the former.

The fable of the twelve labors constituted the sacred
records or scriptures of the older forms of
Astrolatry, one version of which, written with the
cuneiform character upon twelve tablets of burnt
clay, exhumed from the ruins of an Assyrian city,
and now on exhibition in the British Museum, is
ascribed to Nimroud, the prototype of the Grecian
Hercules, and of Nimrod, the Mighty Hunter of the
Old Testament.

ANNIVERSARIES OF SOLAR WORSHIP.

The Nativity.

Applying the anniversaries inculcated in the
worship of God Sol to his imaginary incarnations,
the founders of the ancient Astrolatry made them
refer to the several stages of human existence from

infancy to mature age. Hence, comparing the first day of infantile life to the shortest day of the year, it would naturally be expected that they would have placed the anniversary of the Nativity exactly at the Winter solstice; but, having conceived the idea that the sun stood still for the space of three days at each of the cardinal points, and making it represent the figurative death of the genius of that luminary, they fixed the date for its observance three days later, or on the 25th of December. The Gnostic adherents to the ancient solar worship, or those who were conversant with the teachings of the Esoteric philosophy, knowing that the dramatis personae of the fable of incarnation were pictured with stars upon the azure vault, recognized the woman "clothed with the sun, and the moon under her feet, and upon her head a crown of twelve stars," referred to in Revelations xii. 1, as the Virgo of the Zodiac; they also knew that she was the true queen of heaven and mother of God; and that the infant, anciently represented in her arms, and with whom, in their day, she arose on the Eastern horizon at midnight on the 24th of December, was the same of whom the people were taught to sing at Christmas "Unto us a child is born this day."

With the knowledge of these facts we can readily see that this is the Virgin and child which constituted the originals of those exquisite paintings, by the old masters, known as the Madonna and Child.

Epiphany or Twelfth Day.

In reference to the twelve signs through which the

sun makes his apparent annual revolution, the twelfth day after Christmas, answering to the 6th of January, was observed by the votaries of the ancient Astrolatry as the anniversary of the Epiphany or Twelfth Day. In the solar fables, it was taught that a star appeared in the heavens on that day to manifest the birthplace of the infant Saviour to the Magi or Wise Men of the East, who came to pay him homage, and to present him with the gifts of gold, frankincense and myrrh, as related in Matthew ii. 11.

The reason for presenting these gifts is explained by the facts that of the seven metals dedicated to the genii of the planets, gold was the one consecrated to God Sol; and frankincense and myrrh were the gums burned in censers in his worship.

In reading the account of the Magi's visit to the infant Saviour, we have but to exercise our thinking faculties to realize that it is allegory instead of literal history.

Lent or Lenten Season.

In the ancient solar fables it was taught that the persecutions to which the incarnate Saviours were subjected while passing through the dominion of God Sol as Lord of Evil, raged with greatest fury during the forty days preceding the festival of Easter, which period, beginning when the days were perceptibly lengthening, was called Lent, or the Lenten season. It was during this season that the votaries of the ancient religion were taught to manifest their sympathy for the Saviour in his imaginary conflict with the Devil by abstaining from all festivities, and by fasting and prayer; and, as that was the season in which the flocks and herds were poor in flesh, while the seas and rivers abounded with fish in good condition, the ancient priests, making a virtue of necessity, enjoined a diet principally of fish, and for that reason placed the constellation Pisces at the point in the Zodiac in which the Lenten season anciently began; which, without regard to the day of the week, was always observed on the 15th day of February, the name of that month having been derived from the Februa, or feast of purification and expiation of the old Roman calendar.

At the council of Nice the Lenten season was made to begin on the fourth day of the week, and in reference to the ancient custom of the more devout sprinkling ashes upon their heads at the feast of the Februa, it is called Ash Wednesday.

Hence we see that all years in which Ash Wednesday does not come on the 15th of February, the Lenten season must necessarily contain a greater or lesser number than the original assignment of forty days.

Passion Week.

The last seven days of Lent is called Passion Week, in reference to the apparent passage of the sun across the Celestial equator at the Vernal Equinox or 21st of March; the ancient astrologers having conceived the idea that the sun stood still for the space of three days at each of the cardinal points,

and making it represent the figurative death of the
genius of that luminary, it was observed as the
anniversary of the Vernal crucifixion or passion of
the incarnate Saviours; and in commemoration of
their imaginary sufferings and death it was the
custom to expose in the temples during the last
three days of Passion Week figures representing
their dead bodies, over which the votaries of solar
worship, especially the women, made great
lamentation. It was in reference to one of these
images, laid out in the temple at Jerusalem, to
which the jealous Jehovah, considering it a great
abomination in his own house, is made to direct the
attention of Ezekiel, the prophet, who, looking,
beheld "Women weeping for Tammuz" as recorded
in the eighth chapter. This divinity was the
Phoenician prototype of the Grecian Adonis, to
whom the women of Judea preferred to pay
homage.

It was during the last three days of Passion Week
that the votaries of solar worship performed their
severest penance. Besides fasting and prayer, the
more devout flagellated and slashed themselves and
others with knives and thongs, and carried heavy
crosses up steep acclivities. In all ultra-Catholic
countries the priests, in imitation of the ancient
custom, expose in the churches figures representing
the dead Saviour, over which the laity, especially
the women, weep and mourn; and the more devout
men cut and slash themselves, and each other, with
knives and thongs; and, in imitation of the
imaginary tramp of Jesus with his cross up
Calvary's rugged side, bear heavy crosses up steep
acclivities.

Passion Plays.

Anciently dramas representing the passion of
incarnate saviours, called Passion plays, were
enacted upon the stage. The most celebrated of
these divine tragedies, known as Prometheus
Bound, and composed by the Greek poet
AEschylus, was played at Athens 500 years before
the beginning of the Christian era. To show that this
sin-atoning saviour was not chained to a rock, while
vultures preyed upon his vitals, as popularly taught,
but was nailed to a tree; we quote front Potter's
translation of the play, that passage which, readily
recognized as the original of a Christian song, reads
as follows:

"Lo, streaming from the fatal tree, His all atoning
blood: Is this the infinite? 'Tis he-- Prometheus and
a God. Well might the sun in darkness hide, And
veil his glories in, When God the great Prometheus
died For man, the creature's sin."

The veiling of the sun, as represented in these plays,
having reference to the imaginary sympathy
expressed by God Sol for the sufferings of his
incarnate son, was shown upon the stage by shading
the lights. The monks of the Middle Ages enacted
plays representing the passion of the Christian
Saviour, and the Bavarian peasantry, perpetuating
this custom, perform the play every tenth year.

Resurrection and Easter Festival.

In conformity to the ancient teachings, the incarnate
saviours, considered as figuratively dead for the

space of three days at the Vernal Equinox, or 21st of March, were raised to newness of life after the expiration of that time. Hence, the 25th of March, without regard to the day of the week, was celebrated as the anniversary of the Vernal resurrection. On the morning of this day it was the custom of the astrologers to say to the mourners assembled in the temples, "Be of good cheer, sacred band of initiates; your God has risen from the dead, his pains and his sufferings shall be your salvation." Another form of this admonition, quoted from an ancient poem in reference to the Phoenician Tammuz, reads as follows:

"Trust ye saints, your God restored, Trust ye in your risen Lord, For the pains which he endured, Your salvation hath procured."

Then would begin the festivities of Easter, which corrupted from Eostre, and derived from the Teutonic mythology, was one of the many names given to the goddess of Spring. In the observance of this festival the temples were adorned with floral offerings; the Hilaries sang their joyful lays; the fires upon the pyres, or the fire-altars, were extinguished and rekindled with new fire, or sacred fire of the stars, which the Astrologers taught was brought down from heaven by the winged genius Perseus, the constellation which, anciently, was in conjunction with the Vernal Equinox; Paschal candles, lit from the new fire, were distributed to the faithful and the Paschal feast, Easter feast, or the feast of the passover, was eaten in commemoration of the passion of the incarnate saviours, or, in other words, of the passage of the sun across the celestial equator. In ultra-Catholic countries the descent of the sacred fire is represented by some secretly arranged pyrotechny, and the credulous laity, believing they have witnessed a miraculous display, eagerly solicit Paschal candles lit from it; and in imitation of the ancient festivities in honor of the return of spring, all Catholic churches, and most of Protestant ones, are adorned with flowers, the bells ring out their merriest peals, and "Gloria in Excelsis" and other jubilant songs, similar to the lays of the ancient Hilaries, are sung.

Annunciation.

The anniversary of the Nativity having been placed on the 25th of December, according to the course of nature, the 25th of March was anciently celebrated as the anniversary of the annunciation, and is still observed on that day, and the duty of saluting the Virgin (Virgo) and announcing her conception by the Holy Ghost or third person in the Trinity was assigned to the genius of Spring. In the Chaldean version of the Gospel story the name of Gabriel was given to this personification, and in the Christian version of that story he is made to perform the same office; see Luke i. 26-35.

Ascension.

Celebrating the anniversary of the ascension forty days after Easter, it was anciently observed on the 4th of May, and it was taught that the incarnate saviours ascended bodily into heaven, in a golden chariot drawn by four horses caparisoned with gilded trappings, all glittering like fire in the fervid sunlight. Hence when we read in II. Kings ii. 11, that "There appeared a chariot of fire and horses of fire, . . . and Elijah went up by a whirlwind into heaven," we must accept this text as descriptive of the imaginary ascension of one of the incarnate saviours of ancient Judaism.

Assumption.

When the Summer solstice was in the sign of Cancer, the sun was in that of Virgo in the month of August, and the anniversary of the Assumption was observed on the 15th of that month, and is so observed at the present time. The fact that the anniversary of the Ascension precedes that of the Assumption explains why Jesus is made to say to his mother (Virgo) soon after his resurrection, "Touch me not: for I am not yet ascended to my Father." John xx. 17.

The Lord's Supper.

In the ancient solar worship the so-called ordinance of the Lord's Supper was observed just before the anniversary of the autumnal crucifixion; and consisting of bread and wine, in reference to the maturing of the crops and completion of the vintage, was, like the modern festival of the hardest home, a season of thankfulness to the Lord (God Sol) as the giver of all good gifts. Hence being observed but once a year, it was in reality not an ordinance but an anniversary; and the fact that Christians partake of these emblems so frequently during the year indicates that the original signification of the Lord's Supper has been lost.

Transubstantiation,

or the conversion of the bread and wine into the veritable blood and body of Christ, is a doctrine of the Catholic church which was derived from the ritual of the ancient solar worship.

In the 26th chapter of Matthew we have an account of the Lord administering the last supper to his Disciples on the eve of the autumnal crucifixion, and in verse 27 it reads that "he took the cup, and gave thanks, and gave it to them, saying, Drink ye all of it." The compilers of the modern version of the Gospel story must surely have inadvertently copied this text as it read in the ancient versions of that old, old story, which, when observed in remembrance of "Our Lord and Saviour Bacchus," was called the Bacchanalia, or feast, of Bacchus. At these orgies the participants give thanks for the wine by not only drinking all of one cup, but many more; in fact they kept on drinking until they fell under the table.

Autumnal Crucifixion.

The beneficent seasons of Spring and Summer coming to an end at the Autumnal Equinox, the 22d of September was made the anniversary of the Autumnal Crucifixion. The vernal resurrection and Autumnal Crucifixion, representing the alternate triumph of the personified principles of Good and Evil, as manifested in the diversity of the seasons; we find appropriately expressed in two religious pictures. In the one, the Saviour, appealing as a vigorous young man, surrounded by a brilliant halo, representing the rays of the all-conquering Sun of Spring, is rising triumphantly from the tomb, before whom the demon of Winter, or Devil, is seen retreating in the background. In the other, the vanquished Saviour, represented by the figure of a lean and haggard man, with a crown of thorns upon his head, around which appears a faint halo of the Sun's declining rays, and above which is placarded the letters I. N. R. I., the initial letters of Latin words, signifying the life to come, or the eternal life, is suspended upon the cross, at the foot of which his mother Mary (Virgo) is represented as kneeling in a mourning attitude, and by her side is seen a serpent and a skull, the emblems of Evil and of Death.

Michaelmas.

In the calendar of the ancient Astral Worship, the fourth day after the Autumnal Equinox was dedicated to the genius of Autumn. In the Chaldean allegories the name of Michael was given to this personification, and called Michaelmas, or feast of Michael. In the Catholic calendar this anniversary is placed an the 29th of September, instead of the 26th of that month, while that of St. Matthew, the Christian genius of Autumn, which should be placed on the 26th of that month, is observed on the 21st.

Thus we have shown that the anniversaries of the ancient Astral Worship were all fixed, and from church history we learn that they were so observed

by the Christians until the Council of Nice in the
year 325, when the Bishops assembled at that
celebrated convocation, desiring to have the festival
of Easter celebrated on Sunday, which had been
made the Sabbath by the edict of Constantine, in the
year 321, ordered that it should be observed on the
Sunday of the full moon, which comes on or next
after the Vernal Equinox. Hence, converting it into
a movable festival, its allied feasts and fast days
were also made movable.

PERSONIFICATIONS OF THE DIVISIONS OF TIME.

In the ancient solar fables the several divisions of
time were personified and made to pay homage to
the Triune Deity, supposed to be enthroned above
the firmament.

The Hours.

The genii of the hours were designated as Elders,
and we find them described in the 4th chapter of
Revelation as sitting round about the throne upon
four and twenty seats, clothed in white raiment, and
crowns of gold upon their heads.

The Days.

Each day of the year was appropriately personified,
and these genii of the days constitute the saints of
the Christian calendar. Of these we will refer to but
one. According to the ancient belief that the sun

stood still for the space of three days at each of the cardinal points, the 24th of June was made the first of the decreasing days; and dedicating it to St. John the Baptist, he is made to say in reference to his opposite, (the genius of the 25th of December, and first of the increasing days,) "He must increase, but I must decrease." This text, found in John iii. 30, simply means that the days of the one must increase in length, while the days of the other must decrease.

The Months.

The fable of the twelve labors having been superseded by others, in which the genii of the twelve signs of the Zodiac, corresponding to the months, were designated as angels, and made to minister to God Sol while making his apparent annual revolution; but, when constituted the attendants of the incarnate saviours during their imaginary earth life, they were personified as men and called Disciples. Of these genii of the months we will refer only to the first and the last. The first month, dedicated to the genius known in the mythology as Janus, and from which was derived the name January, was portrayed with two faces, the one of an old man looking mournfully backward over the old year, and the other of a young man looking joyfully forward to the new year. This personification, made the opener of the year, and represented as holding a pair of cross-keys, was called "The carrier of the keys of the kingdom of heaven." Hence, the Popes of Rome, claiming apostolic succession from Peter, the Janus of the Christian twelve, wear cross-keys as the insignia of their office. Sometimes a crosier, or shepherd's crook, is substituted for one of the keys, in reference to his arrogated office of the leader of the sheep! The authority for the assumption that the Popes are Peter's successors is found in Matthew xvi. 18, 19; but its fallacy becomes apparent when we bear in mind that the scriptures are but collections of astronomical allegories, and that the Peter referred to in the text was not a man, but the mythical genius of the month of January.

In reference to the last month, we find that the authors of the ancient solar fables, ever doubting whether God Sol, after inaugurating Winter by his supposed retreat from the earth, would return to revivify nature with his life-giving rays, gave to the genius of the twelfth month the title of the Doubter. In the Christian calendar this personification is known as Thomas, and a more specific dedication of the shortest day of the year having been made to him, the 21st day of December is called St. Thomas day.

The Seasons.

When the cardinal points were in the constellations Leo, Taurus, Aquarius and Scorpio, the astrologers, objecting to the signification of the latter, substituted the constellation in conjunction therewith, which is known as Aquila (Ak-we-la) or Flying Eagle. In the allegorical astronomy of that remote period these genii of the seasons were designated as beasts, and as such we find them referred to in Revelation iv. 7, which reads as follows: "And the first beast was like a lion (Leo), and the second beast like a calf (Taurus, the bull calf), and the third beast had a face as a man, (Aquarius, the waterman) and the fourth beast was like a flying eagle (Aquila)." In the first chapter of Ezekiel, the prophet, the genii of the seasons are referred to in the same manner.

These genii of the seasons, standing, imaginarily, at the four corners of the heavens, were called corner-keepers, and making them witnesses to God Sol in his apparent annual revolution, the founders of the Astral Worship designated them as Archangels, Evangelists, God-Spellers or Gospel-Bearers, and claiming inspiration from them, composed four different histories of the birth and earth-life of the incarnate saviour, to each of which they attached a name, and called these records the Gospel story. In its Chaldean version, the names of Gabriel, Michael, Raphael and Uriel were given them; but while the first two of these are mentioned in the Christian Gospel story, its authors gave to the Evangelists the names of Matthew, Mark, Luke and John. Thus knowing the true signification of the Disciples and Evangelists, the very pertinent question presents itself: If they are not the genii of the months and the seasons, why are there just twelve of the one and four of the other?

Half Year of Increasing Days.

In the ancient astrolatry, the half year of increasing days, extending from the Winter to the Summer Solstice, was personified by the composite figure representing the constellations of Taurus and Aquarius, which, constituted of the winged body of a bull and the head and beard of a man, was called

the Cherubim. This personification we find
portrayed upon the Assyrian marbles on exhibition
in the British Museum.

Half Year of Decreasing Days.

The half year of decreasing days, extending from
the Summer to the Winter Solstice, was personified
by the figure, which, representing the constellations
of Leo and Aquila, and composed of the winged
body and limbs of a lion, with the head of an eagle,
was called the Seraphim. These last two
personifications constituted the Archangels of the
ancient Astral Worship.

Last Quarter of the Year.

The last quarter of the year was personified in the
ancient allegories as a decrepit old man, who, stung
by a Scorpion (Scorpio), and fatally wounded by an
arrow from the quiver of an archer (Saggitarius)
dies at the Winter Solstice; and, after lying in the
grave for the space of three days, is brought to life
again. Such was the personification referred to in
the Christian Gospel-story as having been raised
from the grave by the mandate, "Come forth,
Lazarus." Thus have we shown that the elders and
the saints; the angels, and the Archangels; the
Cherubim and Seraphim; and also poor old Lazarus,
are but personifications of the several divisions of
time.

ZODIACAL SYMBOLS OF SOLAR WORSHIP.

Having shown that the founders of the ancient astrolatry accorded homage to God Sol as Lord of Evil, under the symbol of the serpent, and marked the beginning of his reign, as such, by the constellation "Serpens" placed in conjunction with the Autumnal Equinox; we will now direct attention to the symbols under which he was worshipped as Lord of Good, which, corresponding to the form of the constellation in which occurred the Vernal Equinox, and which was changed to correspond to the form of the succeeding constellation as that Cardinal point passed into it, by that process, known in Astronomy, as the precession of the Equinoxes, its explanation becomes essential to a correct understanding of our subject.

After long observation, aided by the telescope, of which they were undoubtedly the original inventors, the ancient Astrologers discovered that the Sun, in making his apparent annual revolution, did not return to the same point in the heavens, but fell behind that of the preceding year, at the, rate of 50 1/4 seconds of a degree annually. At this rate of precession, which modern, calculation has confirmed, it requires 71 2-3 years for the Cardinal points to pass through one degree on the Ecliptic, and 2150 years through thirty degrees, or one sign of the Zodiac. The knowledge of this process affording an exact chronology, we are enabled, not only to determine the origin of these symbols, but to approximate, very nearly, to the respective dates of their adoption.

The Sphinx.

From the teachings of Astronomy we learn that the Summer Solstice is now occupying the point between the signs of Taurus and Gemini, from which we know that that Cardinal point has passed through three whole signs since it was between the signs of Leo and Virgo, and we have but to multiply 2,150 by 3 to determine that it has been about 6,450 years ago. Hence, the tourist to the Nile valley, when viewing, near the base of old Cheops, the great Egyptian pyramid, a colossal head and bust of a woman, carved in stone, and learns that it is attached to a body, in the form of a lion in a crouching attitude 146 feet long, hidden beneath the shifting sands of the Libyan desert; if possessed of the knowledge of the precession of the Equinoxes, he will be enabled to solve the riddle of the Sphinx by recognizing in that grotesque monument the mid-summer symbol of solar worship, when the Summer Solstice was between the signs of Leo and Virgo.

The Dragon.

When the Summer Solstice was between the signs of Leo and Virgo, the Winter Solstice was between those of Aquarius and Pisces, and the figure composed of the body of a man with the tail of a fish became the mid-winter symbol of solar worship. Such was the form of this symbol to which the ancient Phoenicians paid homage to the Lord under the name of Dagon.

The Bull.

At the same time the Summer Solstice entered the
sign of Leo, the Vernal Equinox entered that of
Taurus, and the bull becoming the spring symbol of
solar worship--the Lord was designated in the
ancient allegories as the bull of God which taketh
away the sin of the world; which, shorn of its
allegorical sense, signifies the sun in Taurus, or sun
of spring, which taketh away the evil of Winter.
Such is the purport of hieroglyphical inscriptions
upon papyrus rolls found in Egypt, and engraved
upon obelisks erected in the Nile valley, one of
which has been recently brought to the City of New
York and set up in Central Park. In the East Indies
this symbol was represented by the figure of a bull
with the solar disk between his horns; and the
Egyptians, who were of Hindoo origin, perpetuating
it in their "Apis," it was reproduced in the golden
calf of the ancient Israelites. The Assyrians
represented this symbol by the figure of a winged
bull with the face and beard of a man; the
Phoenicians, in their "Baal," by the figure of a man
with a bull's head and horns; and the small silver
bull's heads with golden horns, recently discovered
by Dr. Schliemann in the ruins of Mycenae, were
jewels worn by the women of that ancient city,
when the Vernal Equinox was in the sign of Taurus.

The Ram.

By deducting 2,150 years from 6,450, we determine
that about 4,300 years; ago the Vernal Equinox
entered the sign of Aries, and the spring symbol of
solar worship, changing from the bull to the ram,

was represented by ram-headed figures, two of which, found in Egypt, are on exhibition in the British Museum. Then the text which read the bull of God, was changed to the Ram of God which taketh away the sins of the world.

The Lamb.

Ultimately attaching a meek and lowly disposition to the imaginary incarnations of the mythical genius of the sun, the symbol of the ram was changed to that of the lamb, and the text in the allegories, which read the Ram of God, was changed to read "The Lamb of God which taketh away the sin of the World," John i, 29. The explanation we have given relative to the Zodiacal Symbols of solar worship makes the assurance doubly sure that the originals of the New Testament were composed when the Vernal Equinox was in the sign of Aries, as will be shown hereafter. Having adopted the symbol of the lamb, it was represented by several forms of what is known as Agnus Dei, or Lamb of God, one of which was in the form of a bleeding lamb with a vase attached into which blood is flowing, which originated in reference to the shedding of blood as a vicarious atonement for sin. But the most comprehensive form of this symbol in its astronomical signification, was represented by the figure of a lamb in a standing attitude, supporting the circle of the Zodiac, divided into quarters to denote the seasons. At each of the cardinal points there was a small cross, and the lamb held in its uplifted fore-foot a larger cross, the long arm of which was made to cut the celestial equator at the angle of 23 1/2 degrees, the true angle of obliquity of the Ecliptic. This symbol is still retained in the Catholic Church.

The Fish.

By deducting 2,150 years from 4,300 we determine that about 2,150 years ago the Vernal Equinox entered the sign of Pisces; and although the original version of the New Testament was founded upon the symbol of the lamb, it is a historical fact that for centuries after the beginning of our era, the Christians paid homage to the Lord under the symbol of the fish; but ultimately going into desuetude, the lamb was retained as the distinguishing symbol of the Christian religion until the year 680, at which date another was substituted, as will be shown under our next heading.

SIGNS OP THE CROSS.

Among the numerous symbols of solar worship, besides those we have already referred to, there are three to which we will direct attention. Two of these were of astronomical signification: the one adopted when the Spring Equinox was in the sign of Taurus and shaped like the letter T, was the model after which the ancient temples were built; and the other, shaped like the letter X, in reference to the angle of 23 1/2 degrees made by the crossing of the Ecliptic and the Celestial equator, is known as St. Andrew's Cross. The third, and most important of all the symbols of solar worship, in its relation to the Christian religion, which, having no astronomical signification, originated in Egypt, in reference to the annual inundation of the river Nile. To mark the height to which the water should rise to secure an abundant harvest, posts were planted upon its banks to which cross beams were attached thus +. If the water should rise to the designated height, it was called "the waters of life," or "river of life;" and, ultimately, this form of the cross was adopted as the symbol of the life to come, or eternal life; and the ancient astrologers had it engraved upon stone, encircled with a hieroglyphical inscription to that effect, one of which was discovered in the ruins of the temple erected at Alexandria, and dedicated to "our Lord and Saviour Serapis."

But, if the water failed to rise to the required height, and the horrors of starvation becoming the inevitable result, it was the custom of the people to nail to these crosses symbolical personifications of the Demon of Famine. To indicate the sterility of the domain over which he reigned, he was represented by the figure of a lean and haggard man, with a crown of thorns upon his head; a reed cut from the river's bank was placed in his hands, as his unreal sceptre; and, considering the inhabitants of Judea as the most slavish and mean-spirited race in their knowledge, they placarded this figure with the inscription: "This is the King of the Jews." Thus, to the ancient Egyptians, this sign of the cross was blessed or accursed as it was represented with, or without, this figure suspended upon it.

When the Roman, or modern, form of Christianity was instituted, the hieroglyphical inscription signifying the life to come or eternal life was substituted by a placard nailed to the cross with the letters I. N. R. I. inscribed upon it, which are the initials of the Latin words conveying the same meaning. But if we would learn how the figure of a man came to be suspended upon this form of the cross, we must refer to Mediaeval History, which teaches that in the year 680, under the Pontificate of Agathon, and during the reign of Constantine Pogonat, at the sixth council of the church, and third at Constantinople, it was ordered in Canon 82 that "Instead of a lamb, the figure of a man nailed to a cross should be the distinguishing symbol of the Christian religion." Now, as this figure is represented by that of a lean and haggard man, with a crown of thorns upon his head, does it not look as if the old Egyptian Demon of Famine was the model after which it was constructed?

FUTURE REWARDS AND PUNISHMENTS.

In the ancient Astrolatry, two different systems of future rewards and punishments were inculcated; the Oriental or East Indian, and the Occidental or Egyptian; the former, ignoring the resurrection of the body, taught but one judgment immediately after death, and the latter inculcated an individual judgment immediately after death, the resurrection of the body, and a general judgment at the end of the world, or conclusion of the 12,000 year cycle.

The Oriental System.

Considering perfect happiness to consist in absolute

rest, the Oriental astrologers conceived a state of eternal and unconscious repose, equivalent to soul absorption, to which they gave the name of Nirvana, into which they taught that, by the awards of the gods, the souls of the righteous, or those who had lived what they called "the contemplative life," would be permitted to enter immediately after death. But, for the souls of sinners, they invented a system of expiatory punishments which, known as the Metempsychosis, or transmigration of souls, taught that they would be compelled to successively animate the bodies of beasts, birds, fishes, etc., for a thousand years before being permitted to enter the Nirvana.

The Occidental System.

In concocting the doctrine of the first judgment the Egyptian astrologers, ignoring the Nirvana, inculcated the future sentient existence of the soul; and, while retaining the Metempsychotial expiations of the Oriental system, taught that its rewards, and principal punishments, would be enjoyed or suffered in the under or nether world, the existence of which they had conceived in constructing their system of nature. This imaginary region, known to the Egyptians as the Amenti, to the Greeks as Hades, and to the Hebrews as Sheol, was divided by an impassable gulf into the two states of happiness and misery which were designated in the Grecian mythology as the Elysium, or Elysian Fields, and the Tartarus. In the lower part of the latter was located the Phlegethon, or lake of fire and brimstone, the smoke from which ascended into an upper apartment.

In this system it was taught that the souls of the two extremes of society, constituted of the righteous and the great sinners, would be consigned immediately after the first judgment, the one to the Elysium, and the other to the Phlegethon, where they were to remain until the second or general judgment; while the souls of less venial sinners, constituting the greater mass of mankind, before being permitted to enter the Elysium would be compelled to suffer the expiatory punishments of the Metempsychosis, or in the upper region, or "smoky row" of the Tartarus. Such was the Egyptian purgatory, and its denizens constituted "the spirits in prison" referred to in I. Peter iii. 19, from which the astrologers claimed to have the power to release, provided their surviving friends paid liberally for their propitiatory offices; and, from this assumption, the clergy of the Catholic church derived the idea of saying masses for the repose of the soul. These doctrines were carried by Pythagoras from Egypt to Greece about 550 years before the beginning of our era; and passing from thence to Rome, the Greek and Latin poets vied with each other in portraying Hades and the joys and terrors of its two states.

The Second or General Judgment.

The Egyptian Astrologers, recognizing the soul as a material entity, and conceiving the idea that in the future life it would require a material organization for its perfect action, taught that at the general judgment it would be re-united to its resurrected body. In conformity to this belief, Job is made to say in chapter xix. 25, 26, "I know that my Redeemer liveth, and that he shall stand at the latter day upon the earth; and though worms destroy this body, yet in my flesh shall I see God." The higher class Egyptians, however, fearing that their existence would continue to be of the same shadowy and intangible character after the second judgment, as they believed it would be in the Amenti, if worms were allowed to destroy their bodies, hoped to preserve them until that time by the process of embalming.

The imaginary events to occur in connection with the second judgment, which, constituting the finale of the plan of redemption, and inculcated in what are known as the doctrines of Second Adventism, were to be inaugurated by an archangel sounding a trumpet summoning the quick and the dead to appear before the bar of the gods to receive their final awards. At the second judgment, designated in the allegories as "the last day," "day of judgment," "great and terrible day of the Lord," etc., it was taught that the tenth and last saviour would make his second advent by descending upon the clouds, and after the final awards, the elect being caught up "to meet the Lord in the air" (I. Thes. iv. 17), the heaven and the earth would be reduced to chaos through the agency of fire. In reference to that grand catastrophe we find it recorded in II. Peter iii. 10, that "the heavens shall pass away with a great noise and the elements shall melt with fervent heat, the earth also and the works that are therein shall be burned up."

After the organization of a new heaven and a new earth it was taught that upon the latter would descend a beautiful city, with pearly gates and golden streets, called the City of God, the Kingdom of God, the Kingdom of Heaven or New Jerusalem, in which the host of the redeemed would, with their Lord and Saviour, enjoy the Millennium, or thousand years of happiness unalloyed with evil; and such was the Kingdom for the speedy coming of which the votaries of Astral worship were taught to pray in what is known as the Lord's Prayer.

According to the teachings of the Allegories, there were to be no sun, moon or stars during the Millennium, their authors having arranged it so that the light of those luminaries would not be needed, as we find recorded in Rev. xxi. 23, and xxii. 5: "The city had no need of the sun, neither of the moon to shine in it; for the glory of God did lighten it," and "there shall be no night there; and they need no candle, neither the light of the sun; for the Lord God giveth them light." It must be remembered, when reading the fanciful ideas relative to the City of God, that they were composed by men who, living in a very ignorant age, gave free rein to fervid imaginations.

JEWISH OR ANCIENT CHRISTIANITY.

It is our purpose to present the evidences showing that a system of Astral worship, which we designate as Jewish Christianity, was in existence more than two centuries and a half before the institution of its modern form. In verification of this assertion we must find the initial point of our inquiry in ancient history, which teaches that in the division of the

Grecian Empire among his generals, after the death of Alexander the Great, who died 332 years before the beginning of our era, the governorship of Egypt and adjacent provinces was secured by Ptolemy Lagus, or Soter, who, having subsequently suppressed a revolt in Judea, removed from that country a large body of its inhabitants to people the new city of Alexandria, which had been laid out by order of and named after the great Conqueror.

The Egyptian version of the Gospel story, being more appropriate to the Nile Valley than to the region from whence they came, the Greek colonists of Alexandria adopted it, but preferring to pay homage to Serapis, one of the ninth incarnations of God Sol, which they imported from Pontus, a Greek province of Asia Minor, they erected to his worship that celebrated temple known as the Grand Serapium; and, transferring the culture and refinement of Greece to the new city, it became, under the Ptolemian dynasty, a great seat of learning; the arts and sciences flourished, an immense library was collected, the various forms of Astral worship were represented and schools for the dissemination of the several phases of Grecian philosophy and Oriental Gnosticism were founded.

Such being the environment of the Jewish residents of Alexandria, they soon acquired the vernacular and adopted the religion of the Greeks, who, having ever attached to their incarnate saviours the title signifying the Christ, or the anointed, were known as Christians. Encouraged by the liberal policy of Philadelphus, the second Ptolemy, a body of their learned men, who had been educated in the Greek

schools, founded a college for the education of their
own people, which institution was ultimately known
as the University of Alexandria. Under the auspices
of Philadelphus the professors of that institution
rendered their Hebrew sacred records into the
Greek language, which translation is known as the
Septuagint, or Alexandrian version of the Old
Testament.

Having acquired from the Egyptian astrologers the
arts of healing, thaumaturgy and necromancy, and
teaching them in their school, the professors of the
Jewish college of Alexandria assumed the title of
Essenes, or Therapeutae, the Egyptian and Greek
words signifying Doctors, Healers or Wonder
Workers. Possessed of the sad and gloomy
characteristics of their race, they adopted the
"Contemplative Life," or asceticism of the Oriental
Gnosticism, from which they derived the name of
Ascetics. Founding a church for the propagation of
their peculiar tenets, those who were set apart for
the ministry assumed the title of Ecclesiastics.
Inculcating rigid temperance and self-denial among
their people, they were known as Enchratites,
Nazarites or Abstainers; and the more devout
among them retiring to monasteries, or to the
solitude of caves and other secluded places, were
also designated as Monks, Cenobites, Friars,
Eremites, Hermits or Solitaries.

The time having arrived, according to the cyclic
teachings of Astral worship, for the manifestation of
the tenth and last incarnation of God Sol, or, in
other words, to, give a new name to the mythical
genius of the sun, the professors of the Jewish

school of Alexandria is resolved to inaugurate their own form of worship. While retaining the same title under which they had paid homage to Serapis and known as Christians, Essenes or Therapeutae, they substituted for their Christ the name of the Grecian Bacchus, which, composed of the letters {Greek: IOTA,ETA,SIGMA}, signifies Yes, Ies or Jes. In composing their version of the Gospel story, having, like their race, no inventive genius, they appropriated that of Serapis as its basis and laid its scene in the land of their ancestry, but inconsistently retained the sign of the cross and the phraseology connected there with, which, having special reference to the Nile River and its annual inundation, had no application whatever to the sterile land of Judea. Selecting what they conceived to be the best from other versions of the Gospel story, and assuming the title of Eclectics, they designated their system as the Eclectic Philosophy. In proof of the eclectic character of the Gospel and Epistles of ancient Christianity, we refer to the Asceticism inculcated therein, which, derived from the Oriental Gnosticism, we find perpetuated in the scriptures of modern Christianity; we also refer to the miracle of converting water into wine, taken from the Gospel story of Bacchus, and to the statements that the Saviour was the son of a carpenter and was hung between two thieves, copied from the story of Christna, the Eighth, Avatar of the East Indian astrolatry. Thus we see that, although the scene of the Gospel story of ancient Christianity was laid in the land of Judea, its authors having adopted a Greek version of that story as its basis, given a Greek title and name to their Messiah, perpetuated a Greek name for their sect and quoted exclusively from the Septuagint, or Greek version of the Old Testament, the facts show conclusively that it was not Jews of Judea, but Hellenized Jews of Alexandria, who were the real authors of the ancient Christianity.

THE PROPHECIES.

The clergy having ever claimed that the prophecies are Divine revelations of events yet to occur, and having incessantly agitated society by preaching their speedy fulfillment, we propose to expose the fallacy of their teachings by showing that these scriptures are not the records of future events, Divinely reavealed, but that they originated with the founders of Astral worship, who predicated them upon predetermined events of their own concoction, relative to the general judgment, and setting up of the kingdom of heaven, which were to occur as the finale of the plan of redemption and from which were derived the doctrines of second adventism; and, in determining the exact time when then were to occur, we have but to prove that it was coincident with the conclusion of the last half of the grand cycle of 12,000 years, which, as we have shown, was dedicated to man as the duration of his race on earth.

As evidence that the founders of the Jewish or ancient Christianity believed, like the votaries of other forms of Astral worship, that the prophecies were soon to be fulfilled, we find that the New Testament, of the original version of which they were the authors, is replete with such texts as "Repent, for the Kingdom of Heaven is at hand," Matt. iv. 17; "There be some standing here which shall not taste death till they see the Son of Man coming in His kingdom," Matt. xxi. 28; "The time is fulfilled, and the Kingdom of God is at hand," Mark i. 15. That the original version of the New Testament was composed when the Vernal Equinox was in the sign of Aries we are assured by reason of the fact that it inculcates homage to the Lord under the symbol of the Lamb; and that it was during the last, or 30th degree of that sign, can readily be proven by appealing to history and to astronomy, the former of which teaches that the Jews were removed from Judea to Alexandria twenty-five years before the accession to the throne of Philadelphus, the Second Ptolemy, to whom we have referred in our preceding article, and who, after reigning thirty-nine years, died 246 years before the beginning of our era. By reference to the Celestial atlas we will find that the Vernal Equinox will pass out of the sign of Pisces into that of Aquarius, or in the year 1900, and we have but to deduct that period of time from 2150, the number of years required for the cardinal points to pass through one whole sign, to determine that the Spring Equinox passed out of the sign of Aries into that of Pisces 250 years before the beginning of our era, or about 2,100 years ago. Now, from the projections of the astrological science, we are assured that the last half of the grand cycle of 12,000 years, which was allotted to man as the duration of his race on earth, was made to begin at a time corresponding to the Autumnal Equinox, when that cardinal point was passing out of the sign of

Virgo, and that of necessity it had to come to an end at a time corresponding to the Vernal Equinox, when that cardinal point was passing out of the sign of Aries; from which we know why, at the last judgment, the office of trumpeter was assigned to the Archangel Gabriel, the genius of Spring, and why it was a ram's horn with which he was to "toot the crack o' doom"

When the time arrived for the fulfillment of the prophecies we can well imagine that, fearing the wrath of the Lamb, there were weeping, wailing and gnashing of teeth among the terror-stricken sinners, while those who believed they had made their calling and election sure were looking with feverish expectancy for the second advent of their Lord and Saviour; and, doubtless, clothed with their ascension robes, they watched and waited, with ears alert, to hear the sound of Gabriel's trumpet, summoning the quick, and the dead to the general judgment. But not a blast from the archangel's ram's horn was heard reverberating along the skies, no Lord appeared descending upon the clouds to meet the elect in the air, and, in the last act of the fearful drama of "judgment day," the curtain refused to be rung down upon a burning world.

With the non-fulfillment of the prophecies, the more enlightened elements of society began to scoff at the priests, who were temporarily demoralized, but true to their deceptive instincts, soon rallying with the plea of a mistake having been made in the calculations based upon the prophecies, they undoubtedly concocted scripture to meet that very emergency, for, to the taunts of the scoffers who, in reference to the second advent of the Lord, enquired "Where is the sign of His coming? for, since the fathers fell asleep, all things continue as they were from the beginning of creation," they answered that "The Lord is not slack concerning His promise," but "as a thief in the night" he would soon come and all things be fulfilled. See II. Peter, chapter iii.

Following up the history of this interesting subject, we find that the founders of modern Christianity, to which we will refer in our next article, in composing their version of the New Testament from that of the Jewish, or ancient Christians, made no change in its verbiage relative to the prophecies; but when Constantine I., Emperor of Rome, became the patron of the church, her hierarchy, tired of figuring upon them, secured a long respite from that troublesome subject by claiming to have made other calculations, which put off the time of fulfillment to the year 1000; and from history we learn when the time arrived the whole of Christendom was fearfully agitated upon the subject: Since then every generation has been vexed with the fallacies of second adventism; and the facts of the case justify the charge that the clergy, by teaching that the prophecies refer to events yet to occur, are perpetuating a most stupendous fraud upon Christendom, and an earnest and efficient protest should be inaugurated against the further agitation of the monstrous delusion of second adventism, which is frightening thousands of weak-minded people into insanity and causing a vast amount of social distress.

ROMAN OR MODERN CHRISTIANITY.

Having presented the evidences that the Jewish, or
ancient Christianity, originated at the University of
Alexandria, under Greek rule, we now propose to
show that its modern form emanated from the same
source, under Roman rule; but, before entering upon
this investigation, it is important to become
conversant with the sentiments manifested towards
religion by the cultured element of Roman society
in that enlightened era, which, designated as the
golden age of literature, was adorned by such
distinguished orators, philosophers, historians,
poets and naturalists as Cicero, Tacitus, Pliny,
Horace and Virgil. In reference to this subject,
Gibbon, in his history of The Decline and Fall of
the Roman Empire, vol. I., chapter 2, says: "The
various modes of worship which prevailed in the
Roman world were all considered by the people as
equally true, by the philosophers as equally false
and by the magistrate as equally useful. Both the
interests of the priests and the credulity of the
people were sufficiently respected. In their writings
and conversation the philosophers of antiquity
asserted the independent dignity of reason, but they
resigned their actions to the commands of law and
custom. Viewing with a smile of pity and
indulgence the various errors of the vulgar, they
diligently practiced the ceremonies of their fathers,
devoutly frequented the temples of the gods, and
sometimes condescending to act a part on the
theatre of superstition, they concealed the
sentiments of an atheist under the sacerdotal robe.
Reasoners of such a temper were scarcely inclined
to wrangle about their respective modes of faith or

of worship. It was indifferent to them what shape
the folly of the multitude might choose to assume,
and they approached with the same inward
contempt and the same external reverence to the
altars of the Lybian, the Olympian or the Capitoline
Jupiter." Upon the same subject Mosheim, in his
church history, Book I., chapter 1, says that "The
wiser part of mankind, about the time of Christ's
birth, looked upon the whole system of religion as a
just object of contempt and ridicule."

In determining why such adverse sentiments were
entertained towards religion by "the wiser part of
mankind," about the time referred to in the
foregoing quotations, it will be found to have been
owing to the extensive spread of the Esoteric
philosophy, which taught, as previously stated, that
the gods were mythical and the scriptures
allegorical. While attainable only through initiation,
it was necessarily confined to a limited number, but,
ultimately getting beyond the control of the priests
and vast numbers acquiring the knowledge of its
secrets without initiation, it became evident that it
was but a question of time when there would be no
respectable element left to sustain religion. At this
juncture our attention is directed to the University
of Alexandria, which, at that time, was in a
flourishing condition. Having ceased to be an
exclusively Jewish school, students from all parts of
the Roman Empire, without regard to nationality,
were attending it, and its professors were drawn
from the ranks of both Jewish and Gentile scholars.
Realizing the hopelessness of reviving the ancient
faith among the enlightened clement of society, and
the impossibility of proselyting them to a new form

of superstition, these professors resolved to institute a system of worship exclusively for the Jews and the lower and neglected classes of Gentiles, including the slaves and criminals. To that end they rewrote the scriptures of the Jewish or ancient Christianity, which had been preserved among the secret archives of the University. Retaining their teachings relative to the finale of the plan of redemption, and its monasticism; also the land of Judea as the scene of its version of the Gospel story, and the name of its saviour, to which they added the Latin terminal "us," thus making it Iesus or Jesus, they perpetuated the Greek name of Bacchus--the same that was ultimately perverted into the monogram which, consisting of the Roman letters I. H. S., is found in all Catholic churches, and in some Protestant ones, is falsely supposed to stand for Jesus Hominum Salvator, or Jesus, Saviour of Men. Conforming their version of the Gospel story to the lowly condition of its expected votaries, they attached to the saviour the characteristics of poverty, and made it teach that he was born in a manger, that his disciples were but humble fishermen and that the poor would be the only elect in the kingdom of heaven. Dropping the name of Essenes or Therapeutae, and retaining that of Christian, they incorporated a thread of real history corresponding to the reign of Augustus, and arbitrarily made the Christian era begin at that time. Having thus completed their scheme, they prudently destroyed the original from which they compiled their scriptures, and sending out missionaries to all parts of the Empire commissioned them to preach salvation only to the Gentile rabblement and to the Jews.

That the sacred records of the ancient Essenes or Therapeutae constituted the basis of the scriptures of modern Christianity we have the authority of Eusebius, the church historian of the fourth century, from whom we learn nearly all that is reliable of its history during the first three centuries. In his Ecclesiastical History, Book II. chapter 17, he makes the important admission that "Those ancient Therapeutae were Christians, and that their writtings are our Gospels and Epistles." As further evidence that modern Christianity is but a survival of the Eclectic philosophy of the ancient Therapeutae, we have another important admission by the same historian, who, in quoting from an apology addressed to the Roman Emperor, Marcus Antoninus, in the year 171, by Melito, Bishop of Sardis, in Lydia, a province of Asia Minor, makes that apologist say, in reference to certain grievances to which the Christians were subjected, that "the philosophy which we profess truly flourished aforetime among the barbarous nations; but having blossomed again in the great reign of thy ancestor, Augustus, it proved to be, above all things, ominous of good fortune to thy kingdom." Thus we have indubitable evidence that it was the Eclectic philosophy of the Jewish, or ancient Christianity, which "blossomed again," in its modern form, during the reign of Augustus.

From the testimony of Philo, as referred to by Eusebius, and from the writings of Josephus, the Jewish historian, we learn that, at the beginning of our era, the descendants of the ancient Essenes were still observing the practices and customs of monasticism. But as Josephus refers to them only as descendants of the ancient Essenes, and makes no mention of Christ or Christians--except in one paragraph which has been conceded by the best authorities to be an interpolation it is evident that, at that time, they had no connection with the University of Alexandria, and nothing whatever to do with the institution of modern Christianity. It is also apparent that the Jews of Judea had no hand in its organization, for, if they had instituted it, they would not have attached to the Messiah the Greek title signifying the Christ, but, writing their version of the Gospel story in their own dialect, would have used the Hebrew word signifying the Shiloh (see Gen. xlix. 10); and furthermore, having conceived the idea that he would manifest himself as a great temporal prince, who would re-establish the throne of David, and deliver them from the oppression of foreign rulers, they would not have attached to him the humble characteristics of the Christ of the new Testament. Again, if they had been the authors of modern Christianity, it would have been a most surprising inconsistency for them to turn right about and reject its conceptions of a savior, especially when that rejection resulted in the dire persecutions to which their race has ever been subjected by the Christians. But the Gentile riffraff, attracted by the gracious promises of enjoying in the world to come the felicities denied them in this, eagerly attached themselves to the new sect, which rapidly increased in numbers, and its votaries, glorying in the opprobrious epithet of Ebionites, or needy ones, made themselves so obnoxious by their aggression and turbulent dispositions that, barely tolerated by the Government and condemned by the cultured adherents to the established religion, many of them, courting the crown of martyrdom, suffered death at the hands of the civil authorities; and thus was engendered that spirit of hatred against their fancied oppressors which only awaited the opportunity to manifest itself in deeds of rapine and-bloodshed.

The fanacticism which prevailed among the earlier Christians was the direct result of their dense ignorance, and to this sole cause we may ascribe all the trouble which the Roman Government had with them, and to become convinced of this fact we have but to study church history. In reference to this subject Mosheim, in his Ecclesiastical History; Vol. 4, part 2, chap. 1, says: "It is certain that the greatest part both of the bishops and presbyters were men entirely destitute of learning and education. Besides, that savage and illiterate party, who looked upon all sorts of erudition, particularly that of a philosophical kind, as pernicious, and even destructive of true piety and religion, increased both in number and authority. The ascetics, monks and hermits augmented the strength of this barbarous faction, and not only the women, but also all who took solemn looks, sordid garments, and a love of solitude, for real piety, were vehemently prepossessed in their favor." In almost any history of England we will find it recorded that, even in the ninth century, King Alfred lamented that there was at that time not a priest in his dominions who understood Latin; and even for some centuries after the bishops and prelates of the whole Christian community were marksmen, i. e., they supplied by the sign of the cross the inability to write their own names. If the bishops and priests were so supremely ignorant what can he said in reference to the literary attainments of the laity?

The Christians were alternately persecuted and
tolerated by the Roman Emperors until the first
quarter of the fourth century, when certain events
occurred through which the Church of Rome
became the recipient of Imperial Patronage.
Constantine I., called the Great, having made
himself sole Emperor by destroying all other
claimants to the throne, applied to Sopater, one of
the priests of the established religion, for
absolution, and was informed that his crimes were
of such an atrocious character that there was no
absolution for him. Believing that the Phlegethon,
or lake of fire and brimstone, awaited him in the
future life, unless he could obtain absolution, he
became very much distressed when one of his
courtiers, learning the cause and referring him to
the Church of Rome, he at once applied to her
Bishop, Silvester, who, readily granting the desired
absolution, he added another victim to his butcher
bill by ordering the death of the honest priest who
had refused to grant him absolution. The Christian
sect having become a powerful and dangerous
faction, Constantine conceived the idea of
strengthening his usurped and precarious position
by attaching it to his interest, and to that end he
professed himself a convert to its tenets, and, taking
the Church of Rome under his especial patronage,
elevated her Bishop to the rank of a prince of the
Empire and gave him one of his palaces for a
residence.

The Christian hierarchy, knowing that it would be a
potent means of confirming the faith of the laity in

the Gospel story as a literal history to have a tomb of the Saviour to which pilgrimages could be made, and appealing to Constantine to provide one, he sent his mother, Helena, to Judea to find the place and, of course, discovering what she went to look for, he had erected, under her supervision, over the designated spot, that splendid edifice which, known as the church of the Holy Sepulchre, remains to this day. Helena, good at finding lost things, also claimed to have discovered the veritable cross upon which the Saviour had been crucified; and her son, worthy of such a mother, claimed, as recorded by Eusebius, that he had seen with his own eyes the trophy of a cross of light in the heavens, above the sun, bearing the inscription: "In Hoc Signo Vinces," signifying "Under this sign, conquer." Those were times of remarkable and supernatural occurrences.

At the time Constantine became the patron of Christianity the bishops and presbyters of the several churches, seemingly ignorant of the teachings of the Esoteric philosophy relative to the origin of the Trinity, were divided into two factions in discussing the relation between the Father and the Son. One party, headed by Athanasius, a presbyter of Alexandria, and afterwards bishop of that see, advocated the ancient belief that the three persons in the godhead of Father, Son and Holy Ghost is but one God, that Christ is consubstantial or co-eternal with the Father, and that he became man to perform his mission of redemption. Such, in brief, is what is known as the Athanasian or Trinitarian Creed. The other party, headed, by Arius, another presbyter of Alexandria, advocated the belief in one God alone and that Christ, having no existence until begotten of the Father, is not consubstantial or co-eternal with him. Such, in substance, constitutes what is known to the Trinitarian or Orthodox Christians as the Arian or Unitarian heresy. Could stronger evidence be adduced that this controversy was the result of ignorantly making a distinction where there is no difference, for whether Trinitarian or Unitarian the mythical genius of the sun is the God to whom they all paid supreme adoration, although the Christians of to-day would deny it most emphatically.

The faction, advocating the Trinitarian creed having converted the Emperor to their belief, and influencing him to enforce it as a fundamental doctrine of the Christian theology, he, in the year 325, summoned, at his own expense, a general council of bishops and priests to meet at Nice, in Bithynia, a province of Asia Minor. When they had assembled he appeared among them, clad in gorgeous attire, with a jewel-studded diadem upon his royal brow, and, seated upon a gilded chair, presided over their deliberations. A minority of them, holding "most contumaciously" to the Arian heresy, and refusing to change their views at the bidding of the Emperor, he banished them from their respective bishoprics, while the majority adopted the Trinitarian creed, and appealing to Constantine to suppress the writings of Arius he issued an edict for that purpose, which we present as follows: "Moreover we thought that if there can be found extant any work or book compiled by Arius the same should be burned to ashes, so that not only his damnable doctrine may thereby be wholly rooted out, but also that no relic thereof may

remain unto posterity. This we also straightway
command and charge, that if any man be found to
hide or conceal any book made by Arius, and not
immediately bring forth such book, and deliver it up
to be burned, that the said offender for so doing
shall die the death. For as soon as he is taken our
pleasure is that his head shall be stricken off from
his shoulders." Rather a blood-thirsty, edict to be
issued by the "puissant, the mighty and noble
Emperor," and a very inconsistent one, considering
that he soon afterwards readopted the Unitarian
faith and restored the banished bishops to their
respective sees; but, regardless of his action, the
Church of Rome sustained the Trinitarian creed and
enforced the dogma of the supreme divinity of
Christ.

Thus we see that the history of Christianity, in the
first half of the fourth century, cannot be written
without incorporating considerable from the life of
Constantine, whose ensanguined record before his
pretended conversion marks him as the most brutal
tyrant that ever disgraced the imperial purple; but
the appalling crimes he perpetrated afterwards,
among which were the scalding his inoffending
wife to death in a bath of boiling water, and the
murdering, without cause, of six members of his
family, one of which was his own son, justify what
a learned writer said of him, that "The most
unfortunate event that ever befell the human race
was the adoption of Christianity by the crimson-
handed cut-throat in the possession of unlimited
power," and yet Constantine was canonized by the
Eastern church.

During the first three centuries, when Christianity was but a weak sect, her bishops addressed numerous apologies to the Roman Emperors, in which they claimed tolerance from the government on the ground that their form of worship was virtually the same as the established religion. But after Constantine's pretended conversion its hierarchy began to labor for the recognition of Christianity as the state religion, and to give to their demand some show of consistency they insisted that their scriptures were really historical, and that there was no resemblance whatever between the two forms of worship; while theirs was of Divine authenticity the Pagans was purely a human institution.

For centuries after the convocation of the council of Nice the peace and harmony of the several churches were disturbed by the rancorous discussion of the same old questions of Trintarianism and Unitarianism, the Western church adhering to the former while a majority of the Eastern congregations maintained their faith in the latter; but ultimately the Trinitarian party, gaining the ascendency, and persecuting the adherents of the Unitarian faith, the greater part of them retired into northern Arabia where they founded numerous monasteries; and from history we learn that, having impressed their Unitarian faith upon the populace of that country, it was ultimately incorporated into the Koran, the sacred book of Mohammedanism; and, while becoming votaries of that form of worship, still retained the belief that Christ was but one of the prophets.

The cultured adherents to the established form of worship, becoming alarmed at the growing power and influence of the Christians and at the prospect of such an ignorant and vicious rabble obtaining control of the government, regardless of their pledge to keep the Gnosis secret, publicly announced that the Gods were mythical and the scriptures allegorical, and engaged in a heated controversy with the Christians upon the subjects. The character of their discussions is well, although supposititiously, expressed by Gerald Massey, in his work entitled, "The Historical Jesus and the Mythical Christ;" page 179, American edition, where he makes the Gnostics say to the Christians, "You poor ignorant idiots; you have mistaken the mysteries of old for modern history, and accepted literally all that was only meant mystically." To which the Christians responded, "You spawn of Satan, you are making the mystery by converting our accomplished facts into your miserable fables; you are dissipating and dispersing into thin air our only bit of solid foothold in the world, stained with the red drops of Calvary. You are giving a satanic interpretation of the word of revelation and falsifying the oracles of God. You are converting the solid facts of our history into your newfangled allegories;" to which the Gnostics replied, "Nay, it is you who have taken the allegories of Mythology for historical facts."

But it was impossible to stem the rising tide; the lessons which the priesthood had taught the ignorant masses had been too well learned. They were sure that their scriptures were historical; that Jesus Christ was truly the incarnate saviour who

had died and rose again for the salvation of the
elect, and that being the elect it would be pre-
eminently just and proper that the old Pagan form of
worship should be abrogated and theirs recognized
as the state religion. Thus the conflict raged until
the year 381, when, under the reign of the Emperor
Theodosius the Great, this demand having been
formally made, and the Senate, fearing the tumult a
refusal would excite, with a show of fair dealing
ordered the presentation, before that body, of the
respective merits of the two forms of worship. In
that memorable discussion, which lasted a whole
week, Symmachus, a senator, advocated the old
system, and Ambrose, Bishop of Milan, the new,
which resulting, as a foregone conclusion, in the
triumph of Christianity, a decree to that effect was
promulgated.

Then the long deferred opportunity having arrived,
the vengeful bishops, hounding on a no less
vengeful laity, ruthlessly murdered the priests of the
old religion, and, appropriating its emoluments to
their own use, they seized upon its temples, and
demolishing some, converted others into churches.
With iconoclastic hands they destroyed some of the
statues representing the ancient divinities, or after
mutilation exposed others in public places to the
derision of the populace. Subjecting the adherents
to the older form of worship, whom they designated
as infidels, to the most diabolical indignities and
persecutions, they destroyed their works of art,
burned their libraries, suppressed their schools of
learning, and either killed or exiled their professors.
Among the atrocious acts perpetrated by these
fiends in human shape none was more barbarous

than the one committed in Alexandria, in the year 415, when Hypatia, the beautiful and accomplished daughter of Theon, who had succeeded her father as professor of mathematics and philosophy in the Alexandrian University, while on her way to deliver a lecture, was, by order of Bishop Cyril, dragged from her chariot and murdered in a most revolting manner.

One of the successors of Theodosius justified himself in decreeing the spoliation of the old religion upon the grounds that "It was unbecoming a Christian government to supply the infidels with the means of persevering in their errors." Another one of the Emperors, more zealous than his predecessors, decreed the death penalty against all persons discovered practicing any of the rites and ceremonies of the old religion. Thus the onslaught of Christian savagery obliterated the civilization of Greece and Rome, and inaugurated that long reign of intellectual night known as the Dark Ages, which, materially aiding in effecting the decline and fall of the Roman Empire, made it possible to erect upon its ruins that Italian Oligarchy, which, since then, has ruled the greater part of Christendom.

The dogmatic element of the ancient astrolatry, as incorporated into the Christian creed, underwent no material change until the inauguration of the dark ages, when the bishops of the several churches, in the delirium of metaphysical speculation, concocted the previously unheard of doctrine of pre-existence of spirit, in conformity to which God was declared to be purely a spiritual deity, who, existing before matter, created the universe of nothing. Being the sole custodians of the scriptures; and changing the six periods of a thousand years each to the six days of creation, they altered Gen. i, 1, to read, "In the beginning God created the heaven and the earth," which in the original read: "In the beginning, when the Gods (Elohim or Alehim) had made (shaped or formed) this heaven and this earth." These radical changes necessitating others, they made two distinct and independent beings of the principles of Good and Evil personified in the God Sol; the former they embodied in Jesus the Christ and the latter in the Christian Devil, thus supplanting old Pluto; the presiding genius of the under world.

Rejecting the ancient doctrines relative to the soul, and teaching that, having proceeded from a purely spiritual deity, it would exist eternally as an independent spiritual entity, they substituted for the ancient system of limited rewards and punishments the one inculcating their endless duration. These changes in the creed, which were confirmed at the general council of Constantinople, in the year 553, necessitating further alterations of the scriptures, the righteous were promised "eternal life" in the Paradise of God beyond the stars; and, While consigning great sinners to "everlasting punishment" in the Tartarian fires of the under world, the less venial were to expiate their crimes in the same old Purgatory. Thus, having invented an endless heaven and an endless hell for purely spiritual souls, and neglecting to expunge the doctrines of the resurrection of the body, the setting up of the kingdom of heaven upon a reorganized earth and other materialistic teachings of the ancient religion, they made of the creed and scriptures such a conglomeration of "things new and old" that, without the Astrological key, it would be impossible to determine what they originally taught.

At the Reformation in the 16th century Luther and his coadjutors, while projecting into the Protestant creed all the cardinal tenets of Catholicism, excepting that of Purgatory, made no change in the verbiage of the scriptures. Thus retaining the awful doctrine of endless hell, the reformers constructed a creed which they intended for the government of Protestants for all time; but, doing what had never been done before in the history of the world, they gave the scriptures to the laity, and, whether or not they secured the right of private judgment or individual interpretation, it has been taken all the same; and thus opening the door to investigation, it must ultimately result not only in the abrogation of hell, but in the relegation to the limbo of oblivion of the whole dogmatic element of religion.

As a fitting conclusion to this article, we again direct the attention of our readers to the subject of the primary source of religious dogmas. Prior to the establishment of Christianity as the state religion of the Roman Empire, the philosophers who wrote against it invariably made the charge that its theology was derived from the ancient Paganism. After its establishment as the state religion of the Empire, the hierarchy of the church, knowing that this charge was unanswerable, instigated the Emperor Theodosius I. to promulgate an edict decreeing the destruction of all books antagonistic to Christianity. This edict, directed more particularly against the writings of Celsus, was

carried out so effectually that we know nothing of
what he wrote, only as quoted by Origen, the
distinguished church father of the third century,
who attempted to answer in eight books what
Celsus had written in one, entitled "The True
Discourse." In one of his quotations from Celsus'
work he makes that philosopher say "that the
Christian religion contains nothing but what
Christians held in common with heathens, nothing
that was new or truly great." See Bellamy's
translation, chapter 4. During the earlier centuries
the Christians were divided into numerous sects,
entertaining very divergent views, and each faction,
holding all others to be heretical, charged them with
having derived their doctrines from the Pagan
religion. Upon this subject we find that Epiphanius,
a celebrated church father of the 4th century, freely
admits that all that differed from his own were
derived from the heathen mythology. Such was the
position of all orthodox writers during the Middle
Ages, and since the Reformation the Protestant
clergy have uniformly made the same charge
against the Catholic; a few quotations from their
writings we present for the edification of our
readers.

Jean Daille, a French Protestant minister of the 17th
century, in his treatise entitled La Religion
Catholique Romaine Institute par Nama Pompile,
demonstrates that "the Papists took their idolatrous
worship of images, as well as all their ceremonies,
from the old heathen religion." Bishop Stillingfleet
of the English church and a writer of considerable
eminence in the 17th century, said, in reference to
the complaisant spirit of the early church towards

the Pagans, that "it was attended by very bad consequences, since Christianity became at last, by that means, nothing else but reformed Paganism, as to its divine worship." See Stillingfleet's defense of the charge of idolatry against the Romanists, vol. 5, page 459. M. Turrentin, of Geneva, Switzerland, a learned Protestant writer of the 17th century, in one of his orations describing the state of Christianity in the 4th century, says "that it was not so much the Empire that was brought over to the faith, as the faith that was brought over to the Empire; not the Pagans who were converted to Christianity, but the Christians who were converted to Paganism." Thus, having shown that the Catholics derived all their cardinal tenets from the Pagan mythology, the Protestants must surely have obtained theirs from the Catholics, for they teach all of them except that of Purgatory.

FREEMASONRY AND DRUIDISM.

The rites and ceremonies of Astral worship, under the name of Druidism, were primarily observed in consecrated groves by all peoples; which custom was retained by the Scandinavian and Germanic races, and by the inhabitants of Gaul and the British Islands; while the East Indians, Assyrians, Egyptians, Grecians, Romans, and other adjacent nations, ultimately observed their religious services in temples; and we propose to show that the modern societies of Freemasonry, and ancient order of Druids, are but perpetuations of the grove and temple forms of the ancient astrolatry. In determining the fact that Freemasonry finds its prototype in the temple worship of ancient Egypt, we have but to study the Masonic arms, as illustrated in Fellows' chart, in which are pictured, as its objects of adoration, the sun and moon, the seven stars, known as Pleiades in the sign of Taurus; the blazing star Sirius, or Dog-star, worshipped by the Egyptians under the name of Anubis, and whose rising forewarned those people of the rising of the Nile River; the seven signs of the Zodiac from Aries to Libra, inclusive, through which the sun was supposed to pass in making his apparent annual revolution, and which constitutes the Royal arch from which was derived the name of one of its higher degrees; and its armorial bearings, consisting of pictures of the Lion, the Bull, the Waterman, and the Flying Eagle, which representing the signs at the cardinal points, constituted the genii of the seasons. Besides these, we have the checkered flooring or mosaic work, representing the earth and its variegated face, which was introduced when temple worship succeeded its grove form; the two columns representing the imaginary pillars of heaven resting upon the earth at Equinoctial points, and supporting the Royal arch; also the letter "G" standing for Geometry, the knowledge of which was of great importance to the natives of Egypt in establishing the boundaries of their lands removed by the inundations of the Nile, the square and compass, being the instruments through which the old landmarks were restored, and which ultimately became the symbols of justice. The cornucopia, or horn of plenty, denoted the sun in the sign of Capricorn, and indicated the season when the harvest was gathered and provisions laid up for Winter use; the cenotaph or mock coffin with the sign of the cross upon its lid, referred to the sun's crossing of the celestial equator at the Autumnal Equinox, and to the figurative death of the genius of that luminary in the lower hemisphere; whose resurrection at the Vernal Equinox is typified by the sprig of acacia sprouting near the head of the coffin. The serpent, issuing from the small vessel to the left, represented the symbol of the Lord of Evil under whose dominion was placed the seasons of Autumn and Winter; and the figure of a box at the right hand, represented the sacred ark in which, anciently, the symbols of solar worship were deposited; but which is now used by the masons as a receptacle for their papers.

[See plate9.gif]

After, the promulgation, in the fifth century, of the edict by one of the Emperors of Rome, decreeing the death penalty against all persons discovered practicing any of the rites and ceremonies of the ancient religion, a body of its cultured adherents, determining to observe them secretly, banded themselves together into a society for that purpose. With the view to masking their real object, they took advantage of the fact that the square and compass, the plumbline, etc., were symbols of speculative masonry in the temple form of Astral worship, they publicly claimed to be only a trades-union for the prosecution of the arts of architecture and operative masonry; but, among themselves, were known as Free and Accepted Masons or Freemasons. In imitation of the ancient mysteries they instituted lower and higher degrees; in the former they taught the Exoteric creed, and in the latter the Esoteric philosophy, as explained in our introduction. Inculcating supreme adoration to the solar divinity the candidates for initiation were made to personate that mythical being and subjected to the ceremonies representing his figurative death and resurrection, were required to take fearful oaths not to reveal the secrets of the order. To enable them to recognize each other, and to render aid to a brother in emergencies, they adopted a system of grips, signs and calls; and to guard against the intrusion of their Christian enemies they stationed watchmen outside of their lodges to give timely warning of their approach. Thus was instituted the original Grand Lodge of Freemasonry, from which charters were issued for the organization of subordinate lodges in all the principal cities throughout the Roman Empire.

Becoming cognizant of the true object of Freemasonry, the Hierarchy of the Church of Rome resolved to suppress the order, and to that end maintained such a strict espionage upon its members that, no longer able to assemble in their lodges, they determined to defend themselves by an appeal to arms, and gathering together in strongholds, for a long time successfully resisted the armies of the church; but ultimately, being almost exterminated, the residue disbanded, and we hear no more of Freemasonry, as a secret order, until the conclusion of the Dark Ages, when the Reformation, making it possible, a form of the order, recognizing Christianity, was revived among the Protestants; but the Church of Rome, true to her traditions, has never ceased to hurl anathemas against it and all other secret societies outside of her own body. Thus, having made it apparent that Freemasonry, as primarily instituted, was but a perpetuation of the temple form of Astral worship, we can readily see that, while some of its symbols are as old as the ancient Egyptian religion, it did not, as a secret order, take its rise until Christian persecution made it necessary. Hence it cannot justly lay claim to a greater antiquity than the fifth century of the Christian era.

According to Masonic annals a Grand Lodge was organized at York, England, early in the tenth century, but, like the lodges of Southern Europe, was suppressed by the Church of Rome. In 1717 a Grand Lodge was organized at London, England, and soon afterwards the old Grand Lodge at York was revived, and its members took the name of Free and Accepted Ancient York Masons, from which emanated the charter of the Grand Lodge in the United States, which was organized in Boston in 1733. In 1813 the rivalry between the Grand Lodges of York and London was compromised, and the supremacy of the former was conceded.

From church history we learn that in the year 596 of our era Pope Gregory I. dispatched Augustin, and forty other monks of the order of St. Andrew, from Rome to Britain, to convert the natives to Christianity; but, while the Anglo-Saxons embraced the new faith, the Britons rejected it, and, being persecuted by the Christians, retired to the fastnesses of the country known as Wales, where, for a long period, they maintained the observance of the Druidical form of worship; and although that country has long since become Christianized, the society of the Ancient Order of Druids has existed with an uninterrupted succession at Pout-y-prid, where the Arch-Druid resides, and from, whence emanated the charter of the Grand Lodge of the order in this country. In reference to the Druidism on the continent, history records the fact that when one of the reigning kings became a convert to Christianity the whole of his subjects were baptized into the Church of Rome by Imperial decree.

THE SABBATH.

In determining the origin of the seventh day Sabbath, we must of necessity refer to that source of all religious ordinances, the ancient astrolatry, the founders of which, having taught that God Sol was engaged in the reorganization of Chaos during the first six periods of the twelve thousand year cycle, corresponding to the months of Spring and Summer, they conceived the idea that he ceased to exert his energies, or rested from his labors on the seventh period, corresponding to the first of the Autumn months. Hence, deriving the suggestion from the apparent septenary rest in nature, they taught that God ordained the seventh day of the week as the Sabbath or rest day for man.

In conformity to this ordinance the founders of ancient Judaism enforced the observance of the seventh day Sabbath in the fourth commandment of the Decalogue, which, found in Gen. xx. 8-11,[1] reads as follows, viz: "Remember the Sabbath day to keep it holy. Six days shalt thou labor and do all thy work; but the seventh day is the Sabbath of the

Lord thy God; in it thou shalt not do any work, thou, nor thy son, nor thy daughter, thy man servant, nor thy maid servant, nor thy cattle, nor thy stranger that is within thy gates; for in six days the Lord made heaven and earth, the sea and all that in them is, and rested the seventh day; wherefore the Lord blessed the Sabbath day and hallowed it." Thus was the seventh day of the week made the Sabbath of the Old Testament; but the authors of the Jewish or ancient Christianity, looking for the immediate fulfillment of the prophecies relative to the second judgment, ignored its observance, as may be seen by reference to Mark ii. 23, 27; John v. 2-18; Romans xiv. 5; and Col. ii. 16; and the founders of modern Christianity, perpetuating the belief in the speedy fulfillment of those prophecies, made no change relative to the Sabbath in their version of the New Testament.

After Constantine's pretended conversion to Christianity, and the time for the fulfillment of the prophecies had been put off to the year 10000, as previously stated, the hierarchy of the church appealed to the Emperor to give them a Sabbath, and although they knew that the seventh day of the week was the Sabbath of the Old Testament, and that Sunday was the first of the six working days, according to the fourth commandment, their hatred to the Jews for refusing to accept their Christ as the Saviour induced them to have it placed on the first day of the week. Hence that obliging potentate, in the year 321, promulgated the memorable edict, which, found in that Digest of Roman law known as the Justinian Code, Book III., Title 12, Sec. 2 and 3, reads as follows, viz.: "Let all judges and all people of the towns rest and all the various trades be suspended on the venerable day of the Sun. Those who live in the country, however, may freely and without fault attend to the cultivation of their fields lest, with the loss of favorable opportunity, the commodities offered by Divine Providence shall be destroyed." Thus we see that the primary movement towards enforcing the observance of Sunday, or Lord's Day, as the Sabbath, did not originate in a Divine command, but in the edict of an earthly potentate.

This edict was ratified at the third council of Orleans, in the year 538; and in order, "that the people might not be prevented from attending church, and saying their prayers," a resolution was adopted at the same time recommending the observance of the day by all classes. From merely "recommending," the Church of Rome soon began to enforce the observance of the day; but, in spite of all her efforts, it was not until the 12th century that its observance had become so universal as to receive the designation of "The Christian Sabbath."

Cognizant of the manner in which Sunday was made the Sabbath, Luther issued for the government of the Protestant communion the following mandate: "As for the Sabbath, or Sunday, there is no necessity for keeping it;" see Michelet's Life of Luther, Book IV., chapter 2. Luther also said, as recorded in Table Talk, "If anywhere the day (Sunday) is made holy for the mere day's sake; if anywhere anyone sets up its observance upon a Jewish foundation, then I order you to work on it, to dance on it, to ride on it, to feast on it, and to do anything that shall reprove this encroachment on the Christian spirit of liberty." Melancthon, Luther's chief coadjutor in the work of Reformation, denied, in the most emphatic language, that Sunday was made the Sabbath by Divine ordainment; and in reference thereto John Milton, in reply to the Sunday Sabbatarians, makes the pertinent inquiry: "If, on a plea of Divine command, you impose upon us the observance of a particular day, how do you presume, without the authority of a Divine command, to substitute another in its place?"

During the reign of Elizabeth, Queen of England, a sect of fanatics, known as Dissenters or Nonconformists, basing their action upon the fallacious arguments derived from the fourth commandment, and upon the plea that the Saviour was raised from the dead on the first day of the week, inaugurated what is known as the Puritan Sabbath, which having been transferred to our shores by the voyagers in the Mayflower, and enforced by those statutory enactments known as Blue Laws, caused the people of New England to have a blue time of it while the delusion lasted; and now a large body of Protestant clergy perverting the teachings of scripture, and, ignoring the authority of the Reformers, are disturbing the peace of society by their efforts to enforce the code of sundry laws, which were enacted through their connivance. Thus have we shown that, originating with the Catholics and adopted by the Protestants, the Sunday Sabbath is purely and entirely a human institution, and, being such, we must recognize all Sunday laws as grave encroachments upon constitutional liberty; and it behooves the advocates of individual rights to demand their immediate repeal; for unless a vigilant watch is kept upon the conspirators who secured their enactment, our fair land will soon be cursed by a union of church and State, the tendency in that direction having been indicated by the unprecedented opinion recently handed down by one of the Justices of the United States Supreme Court that this is a Christian Government.

PIOUS FRAUDS.

By claiming to be divinely appointed for the propagation of a divinely authenticated religion, the priesthood of all forms of worship have ever labored to deceive and enslave the ignorant multitude; and in support of these fallacious assumptions have resorted to all manner of pious frauds, in reference to which we quote from both Pagan and Christian sources with the view to showing that the moderns have faithfully followed the ancient example. Euripedes, an Athenian writer, who flourished about 450 years before the beginning of our era, maintained that, "in the early state of society, some wise men insisted on the necessity of darkening truth with falsehood and of persuading men that there is an immortal deity who hears and sees and understands our actions, whatever we may think of that matter ourselves." Strabo, the famous geographer and historian of Greek extraction, who flourished about the beginning of the Christian era, wrote that "It is not possible for a philosopher to conduct by reasoning a multitude of women and the low vulgar, and thus to invite them to piety, holiness and faith; but the philosopher must make use of superstition and not omit the invention of fables and the performance of wonders. For the lightning and the aegis and the trident are but fables, and so all ancient theology. But the founders of states adopted them as bugbears to frighten the weak-minded." Varro, a learned Roman scholar, who also flourished about the beginning of our era, wrote that "There are many truths which it is useless for the vulgar to know, and many falsehoods which it is fit that the people should not know are falsehoods."

So much from Pagan authorities relative to the necessity of deceiving the ignorant masses. We will now present some Christian authorities upon the same subject; and first from Christ himself, who in addressing his disciples is made to say, in Mark iv, 11, 12, "Unto you it is given to know the mystery of the kingdom of God; but unto them that are without all these things are done in parables, that seeing they may see and not perceive; and hearing they may hear and not understand." Paul, in his fourteen Epistles, inculcates and avows the principle of deceiving the common people. He speaks of having been upbraided by his own converts with being crafty and catching them with guile and of his known and wilful lies abounding to the glory of God. See Romans iii. 7, and II. Cor. xii. 16. If Christ and Paul were guilty of deception, their followers had good excuse for the same course of conduct. Upon this subject Beausobre, a very learned ecclesiastical writer, who flourished about the beginning of the 18th century, says: "We see in the history which I have related a sort of hypocrisy that has been, perhaps, but too common at all times; that churchmen not only do not say what they think, but they do say the direct contrary of what they think. Philosophers in their cabinets; out of them they are content with fables, though they well know that they are fables." Historie de Manichee, vol. 2, page 568. Bishop Synesius, the distinguished author of religious literature and Christian father of the 5th century, said: "I shall be a philosopher only to myself, and I shall always be a bishop to the people." Mosheim, the distinguished author of Ecclesiastical History, Vol. I., page 120, says: "The authors who have treated of the innocence and sanctity of the primitive Christians have fallen into the error of supposing them to have been unspotted models of piety and virtue, and a gross error indeed it is, as the strongest testimonies too evidently prove." The same author, in Vol. I., page. 198, says in the fourth century "it was an almost universally adopted maxim that it was an act of virtue to deceive and lie, when by such means the interest of the church might be promoted." In his Ecclesiastical History, Vol. II., page 11, he says that "as regards the fifth century, the simplicity and ignorance of the generality in those times furnished the most favorable occasion for the exercise of fraud; and the impudence of impostors in contriving false miracles was artfully proportioned to the credulity of the vulgar; while the sagacious and the wise, who perceived these cheats, were overawed into silence by the dangers that threatened their lives and fortunes if they should expose the artifice." Thomas Burnet, D.D., who flourished about the beginning of the 18th century, in his treatise entitled De Statu Mortuorum, purposely written in Latin that it might serve for the instruction of the clergy only, and not come to the knowledge of the laity, because, as he says, "too much light is hurtful for weak eyes," not only justifies, but recommends the practice of the most consummate hypocrisy, and that, too, on the most awful of all subjects; and would have his, clergy seriously preach and maintain the reality and eternity of hell torments, even though they should believe nothing of the sort themselves. See page 304. Hugo Grotius, the eminent writer of Holland in the 17th century, says in his 22d Epistle: "He that reads ecclesiastical history, reads nothing but the roguery and folly of bishops, and churchmen." In the language of Robert Taylor, from whom we have taken most of the quotations under this heading, we assert that "no man could quote higher authorities," to prove "the roguery and folly of bishops and churchmen."

CONCLUSION.

Having presented the evidences in support of the
apparently untenable assertion that, notwithstanding
the numerous modes in which man has manifested
his devotional proclivities, the world has virtually
had but the one religion founded in the worship of
personified nature, we are necessitated to recognize
the facts that the Christian Scriptures like the sacred
records of other forms of nature worship are, but a
collection of astronomical allegories; that the gospel
story is truly "the old, old story" which had been
told of a thousand other Saviours before it was
applied to the Christian Messiah; that Jesus is but
one of the many names given to imaginary
incarnations of the mythical genius of the sun; and
that the Disciples and Evangelists are but the genii
of the months and the seasons. Such being the facts,
which cannot be successfully refuted, we must
believe that the Christian religion, instead of being
of Divine authenticity, as popularly claimed, is
purely and entirely of human origin, and that all its
teachings relative to a future state are but priestly
inventions, concocted for the purpose of enslaving
the ignorant masses.

When we think of the thousand millions of dollars
invested in church properties, and estimate the cost
of maintaining more than a hundred thousand
priests and ministers, in supporting foreign and
domestic missions and in publishing religious
literature; besides the taxes applied to the care of
the religious insane, and realize the fact that all of
this vast sum of money is abstracted from the
resources of the people, we would not have to go

outside of our own country to appreciate the fact that religion is the burden of all burdens to society; and when we contemplate the great disturbance to the social relation, resulting from sectarian strife, and the almost universal disposition of Christians to persecute and ostracize those who differ with them in opinion, we can readily subscribe to the sentiment accredited to one of our revolutionary sires, that "this would be a good world to live in if there was no religion in it."

If the clergy had been laboring as faithfully to impress the observance of ethical principles as they have to indoctrinate the people with the superstitions of religion, we would not now be deploring the great demoralization of society. It is a grave arraignment of the clericals to charge them with being, indirectly, the cause of this lamentable state of things; but it is a condition that might have been expected, for, when entering the ministry, they engaged themselves, not so much to teach ethics as to propagate faith in the doctrines of their respective sects. Thus hampered they cannot do the good to society their better natures might desire. Hence the only hope for improvement is for the people to wholly ignore the dogmatic element of religion, and refusing to longer support it, demand that moral training shall be the grand essential of education. If this course were adopted and persistently followed, it would be but a question of time when mankind would come into being with such a benign heredity that crime would be almost impossible.

Then, since religion inculcates a salvation that does not save, let us rise superior to its false teachings and, accepting science as the true saviour of mankind, find our whole duty in the code of natural morality, the spirit of which is embodied in that comprehensive precept known as the golden rule, which, being the outgrowth of the discovered necessities of association, without which society could not exist, it necessarily constituted man's sole rule and guide long before priest or temple; and founded in the eternal principles of right, truth and justice must remain as man's sole rule and guide when priest and church are numbered among the things that were. Spirit of progress! speed the day when all mankind, redeemed from the bondage of superstition, will recognize the great truth that nature, governed by her own inherent forces, is all that has been, all that is and all that shall be; and that, ceasing to indulge in the vain hope of a blissful immortality in a paradise beyond the stars, will make a real paradise of this old earth of ours.

60232563R00056

Made in the USA
Lexington, KY
01 February 2017